How to Play Baseball
Better Than You Did Last Season

ILLUSTRATED BY KEVIN CALLAHAN

Jonah Kalb

How to Play
Baseball
Better Than You
Did Last Season

MACMILLAN PUBLISHING CO., INC.
New York
COLLIER MACMILLAN PUBLISHERS
London

Macmillan Publishing Co., Inc.,
866 Third Avenue, New York, N.Y. 10022
Collier-Macmillan Canada Ltd.
Library of Congress catalog card number: 73–582
Printed in the United States of America

10 9 8 7 6 5 4 3 2 1

Library of Congress Cataloging in Publication Data

Kalb, Jonah.
    How to play baseball better than you did last season.
    1. Baseball—Juvenile literature.   [1. Baseball]
I. Callahan, Kevin, illus.   II. Title.
GV867.5.K34   796.357   73–582   ISBN 0–02–749330–X

Dedication and Acknowledgment

This book is dedicated to the Lexington (Massachusetts) Red Sox, of the 1971 and 1972 seasons, who had one second place finish and one American League (and town) championship . . . their manager, Mr. John Leonard . . . my fellow coaches, Mr. John Morgenstern and Mr. John Holdsworth . . . and twenty-one superkids who were everything those years: Jeremy Bradshaw, Dave Chirokas, Andy Cohen, Jeff Cohen, Chip Holdsworth, Danny Morgenstern, Rick Murphy, Tom Riley, Danny Rosa, Steve Ross, Bob Rubinovitz, Bob Schelling, Brad Schulz, Dave Scott, Dave Semon, Neil Shapiro, Peter Simeone, Bob Tillinghast, Mark Trantanella, Bobby Walsh . . . and most especially, Gene Kalb. Were it not for Gene, this book would never have been written.

I wish to acknowledge the advice and suggestions of Coach John Morgenstern, many of whose ideas have found expression in this book.

Contents

How to Play Baseball
Better Than You Did Last Season

Introduction

This is a manual about how to play baseball better than you did last year. It gives you some basic information, hints on how to improve, tips on what to practice, and suggestions not only for you but for the whole team. The best way to use this manual is for every player on your team to read and understand the whole book, and then practice. The next best way is for each player to study those sections of the book which concern him.

Most players play more than one position. That is why it is a good idea for all players to know something about all positions. If you are a very good ballplayer, you will probably get picked for an all-star team some time. All-star teams usually end up with nine pitchers and seven shortstops, and so a lot of very good ballplayers don't do well because they end up playing positions they never tried before and don't know anything about. If they read about and understand *all* positions, they will be more valuable to the all-star team.

1

You should read the book anyway. Even if the rest of the team never reads or even hears of this manual, you will be a better ballplayer if you read it and practice your skills. You don't even have to belong to a team. Baseball is a team sport, but it is also an *individual* sport. The best teammates in the world won't help you hit—only you can do it. Nobody can help you when that fly ball is hit in your direction. You have to make the catch by yourself.

Play other sports. Basketball is a good game for baseball pitchers. It gives you a lot of wind sprints and builds up your legs. Hockey is excellent for baseball players because good hockey playing builds stamina. Football is good for teamwork, tennis for eye-hand coordination, badminton for pop-ups, and track for speed and stamina. Every sport helps you be a better baseball player and makes you stronger—so play.

Practice in the winter. This manual has many suggestions for things you can do in your basement during the winter to make you a better baseball player the following season.

This manual is written in sections. If you can't read everything in it, then read just the sections that apply to you. Every player should read the sections on Hitting, Base Running, and Coaching. Then, depending on what position you think you will probably play, here is a *minimum* number of sections to read:

Catchers should read General Infielding, Pitching, and Catching. Pitchers should read General Infielding and Pitching. Basemen should read General Infielding and the section that deals with their particular base. Outfielders should read General Outfielding and the section that deals with their particular position.

And now, play ball. But before you do . . .

Wear a long-sleeved sweatshirt under your uniform. Your sweatshirt should at least cover your elbows. In warm weather, you may wear a lighter weight long-sleeved shirt, but you must protect your elbows when sliding. (Pitchers, incidentally, may not wear sweatshirts with white or frayed sleeves. It is too difficult for the hitters to see the ball, and it is against the rules.)

Wear a cup. It does not interfere with your playing or your running.

3

Don't drink anything during the game, not even water. You may get thirsty, but water slows you down and can give you cramps or upset your stomach. If you get unbelievably thirsty during the game, wash your mouth out with water. You may take *one sip*, but it's best not to take anything.

During the game, you belong on the bench or in the field. Don't horse around or talk to people in the stands. You belong in the field or on the bench, paying attention to the game.

Don't wear a jacket in the game. Sometimes you play baseball when it's cold. You may wear a jacket on the bench but you are not allowed to wear one in the field or at bat. You can't move your arms freely with a jacket. If you need to, wear a sweater *under* your uniform in addition to your sweatshirt. Try to keep your hands warm before you bat. (You can wear regular gloves on the bench, but not at bat.)

During a game or practice, talk baseball to your teammates, but never criticize them. Cheer your teammates on, slap them on their backs, yell encouragement. On the bench, analyze what the pitcher is throwing. In the field, chatter, encourage your teammates, cheer. But you should not criticize your teammates in any way.

You should not say anything to the umpire. You may ask him a question, like "how many outs?"

4

but you should not argue with him. Even if he is wrong you should not voice any complaints. If you think the umpire made a mistake in the *rules*, tell your manager before the next pitch. He will discuss it with the umpire. If you think the umpire made a bad judgment, forget it. Your coach probably won't even discuss it.

Don't call yourself out. Sometimes an umpire will make a mistake and call you *safe* when you know you were really out. Don't argue or correct him on this kind of call either. *Just don't take your foot off the base!* His bad calls will probably even out in the course of the game. This is *not* cheating or being dishonest. Expect umpires to make both favorable and unfavorable mistakes.

You should not say anything at all to the other team. You should not ride the pitcher, tease the other team's players, or make noise to rattle them. You can congratulate someone on the other team for a good play. But in general, you should not say *anything* to the other team during a game. After the game, since many of these boys are your friends, say what you like.

Don't worry about your errors. Nobody will criticize you for them—not even the coaches. Everybody makes errors, so forget them and go on to the next play. If you look as if you're worrying about an error, the coach may pull you out of the game. Worried ballplayers tend to make *more* mistakes.

Stay alert for signals. Many teams use signal systems for stealing, bunting, taking pitches, and so forth. These signals are almost always given by the third base coach, but most of the time he gets his orders from the manager. If you get a signal, follow it *immediately*, even if it seems wrong to you. You have no choice.

Don't listen to the fans. Sometimes you get a lot of advice from the people in the stands. Don't listen to them, even if the advice is coming from your parents. When on the field, the manager and coaches run the team. Take all your instructions from them.

Hitting

Hitting is the most natural baseball skill. Some hitters seem to have been born with a natural ability to hit. But there is a lot that can be learned about hitting. When you hit, you use your bat, your arms, your legs, your feet, your hands, your eyes, and your body. But you also hit with your brains—and that is the area that keeps improving with experience.

Pick a bat that you can swing quickly. This usually means picking a bat one size smaller than you think you like. Speed of bat is a lot more important in getting hits than weight of bat.

"Get the bat on the ball." If there is one thing going through your mind when you're hitting, it should be this phrase. Do anything you can to *get the bat on the ball.*

Hitting the ball fair will get you on base 50 per cent of the time. When you hit fair balls, some will be hits, some the fielder will miss, ground balls hit stones, infielders will make bad throws, first basemen will drop throws, players drop pop-ups, some will drop fly balls, others throw to the wrong base, and some will fall down. You can hit only .250 but be worth .500 to your team because you always hit the ball fair.

The Form of Hitting

Your feet should be in the proper position in order to hit. They should be comfortably apart and parallel to the edge of home plate. With knees slightly bent, get up on the balls of your feet and lean a bit toward the plate. You cannot get the power or the stride to hit if you're standing back on your heels. So get on the balls of your feet, then shift your weight to your back foot. As you swing, transfer your weight to your front foot.

Your distance from the plate should be about fifteen to twenty-four inches. When measuring remember that you want the barrel of your bat—the fat part—over the plate when you swing. Some hitters lean over and touch their bats to the far edge of the plate. When they straighten up and swing level, the fat part of the bat covers the middle of the plate.

Choose the position in the batter's box that's best for you. Most hitters put their back foot on the back line of the batter's box—especially for fast ball pitchers. Some hitters move all the way up to the front of the box for slow ball or curve ball pitchers. Others stay right in the middle of the box. Stand where you feel most comfortable.

Setting the bat and your hands is important to good batting form. Hold the bat in such a way that when it crosses the plate during your swing, the label will be facing straight up or straight down. Place your hands with the two sets of knuckles of one hand lined up with the two sets of knuckles of the other—right hand above left hand if you're right-handed, left hand above right hand if you're left-handed. Keep both hands together, an inch or so above the knob of the bat handle. Then move your hands to a position in front of your back shoulder (or slightly lower) holding the bat straight up in the air, or possibly pointing slightly backward. Keep your back elbow away from your body, and do not lean the bat on your shoulder. Cock your wrists. This is the "classic" batting stance, but you may change it slightly if you feel more comfortable some other way.

Keep your eyes on the ball all the way to the bat. It's very hard to keep your eyes on the ball from the moment it leaves the pitcher's hand until it hits your bat, but if you learn to do it you will be a good hitter. Practice it. When you let a pitch go by, you should watch it all the way to the catcher's mitt. *Concentrate hard on the ball.* As you watch the ball coming in, try to see the seams. Count the stitches on the seams. See if you can tell which way the ball is spinning. None of this will help anything except your concentration, but if you're counting seams and stitches, your eyes will be on the ball.

You need quick hands to hit well. In the middle of your swing, just when you are about to hit the ball, you have to "explode" your hands and wrists. Here is an example to let you know what that means. If you are a right-handed hitter, hold your left arm up and pretend there is a fly on your arm. Take your right hand (without the bat, of course), sneak up on the imaginary fly, and then, as it flies away, grab for it with your right hand. Notice what your hand has to do. *You use the same motion* of "exploding" your hands when you swing a bat.

Always swing level. Do not swing up at the ball. To practice this, pretend you are throwing the barrel of your bat right at the pitcher's chest. Don't let go of the bat, of course, but if you *did* let go, the bat should hit the pitcher right in the chest. If you do that, you will be swinging level.

Stride right at the pitcher. As you swing, stride with your forward foot toward the pitcher. Do not "step in the bucket" away from the pitcher. Your swing should open up your hips so that you are almost facing the pitcher.

Adjust your swing up or down. If you find yourself swinging above the ball, next time swing a little lower than you think you should. If you find yourself swinging under the ball, swing a little higher than you think you should.

If you're swinging late, choke up. Some coaches tell all young hitters to choke up two or three inches on the bat. This means sliding both hands up the handle of the bat two or three inches. Some coaches say to *always* choke up when you have two strikes against you. The reason most right-handed hitters hit to right field is that they are not strong enough to get the barrel of the bat around in time. Get a lighter bat, or choke up on it, or do both. Then "throw" the barrel of the bat at the pitcher.

Hit the ball when it's out in front of you. Get the bat on the ball when it is six inches or a foot in front of home plate, not over home plate. You can see the ball better there. And if you hit it, it will go down your power alley (left field or left center if you are a right-handed hitter).

Follow through smoothly. Don't stop your swing. It is very important to keep going all the way around, whether you hit the ball or not. Good follow-through helps you hit *through* the ball, and it gives you all your distance and power.

If you're having trouble hitting, shorten your backswing. Swing less hard, and don't start your swing so far back. If necessary, wait for the pitch with your bat pointing directly at the catcher. Remember, nothing else matters unless you can *get the bat on the ball.*

Swing a bat with a "donut" when on deck. If you don't have a donut or a leaded bat, swing two bats together. The purpose of this is to tense the muscles in your arms. If you first swing a weighted bat, your regular bat will feel light by comparison. You will then be able to swing it more quickly.

Remember the basics of hitting form. Get on the balls of your feet, leaning forward; your hands, with knuckles lined up, should be in front of your back shoulder. Concentrate so hard that you can count the stitches on the ball. Swing level, "explode" your hands, "throw" the bat at the pitcher, and follow through. But most important, *get the bat on the ball.*

The Brainy Part of Hitting

Know what kind of pitch you can hit best. Nobody can hit all kinds of pitches equally well. If someone says he can hit "anything," he's probably getting a lot of poor hits. In batting practice and in games, see what kind of pitches you hit best— not the pitches that you hit grounders on, but the ones you hit for line drives most often. Study yourself. *The kind of pitch you hit best becomes "your pitch."* It's the one that you can almost always hit for line drives. Remember it. Think of it. And in most cases in youth baseball, *you can wait for it.*

If the count is in your favor, don't swing at anything that isn't "your pitch." If you hit waist-high fast balls best, and if the pitcher gets behind you on the count—say, two balls, no strikes, or three balls, one strike, or even one ball, no strikes— *never swing at anything that isn't "your pitch."* A good hitter, with the count three balls, one strike, who swings at a strike around his knees will usually hit a ground ball. If he lets it go, it is three and two, but the next pitch may be just where he wants it. If you are ahead on the count and you know you won't swing at anything except "your pitch," *set up for it.* Say to yourself, "Here comes my waist-high fast ball," and get ready to hit it. If it isn't what you are set up for, let it go. If it *is,* then swing.

BALLS	STRIKES
0	0
1	0
2	0
2	1
3	1

SWING AT
" YOUR PITCH "
ONLY

Hitting "your pitch" is worth at least 150 points to your batting average. It's the difference between a .200 hitter and one who hits .350, or a .500 hitter hitting .650. And it may mean winning a few ball games.

You don't have to swing just because it's a strike. With less than two strikes, you can afford to *take* a strike. The next pitch may be juicy. Don't let your pride interfere with your hitting. If the pitcher fools you, get the next one. Don't try to prove you can hit "anything."

BALLS	STRIKES
0	2
1	2
2	2
3	2

CHOKE UP, SWING AT <u>ANY</u> STRIKE

If you have two strikes on you, protect the plate. If the pitcher has two strikes on you, shorten your swing, choke up a little on the bat handle, and be ready to swing at anything that is a strike. If you think the pitch is almost a strike, you'd better swing at it. Don't take any chances on being called out.

Never swing at a pitch that isn't a strike. Nobody hits bad pitches well. If it's not a strike, forget it. A good hitter walks a lot because he never swings at a bad pitch, nor does he always swing at every strike.

You only need one pitch to hit. *Think about how many you have left.* When you go up to the plate, the pitcher will have to get three pitches past you to get you out. After he has a strike on you, you still have two left. Even with two strikes on you, he has to get one more past you. If you look at it that way, and if you remember that you want a *hit* (not a ground ball, not a pop-up, but a hit), you

14

won't swing at a pitch you can't hit well because you would be giving up the pitches you have left—some of which might be just what you want.

Don't ever let a pitcher throw a pitch when you're not ready. You should be set up in your correct stance and mentally ready, too. If you need time to do this, step out of the box—for every pitch if you have to. The umpire will give you all the time you need.

Think about what the pitcher will throw next. If the last pitch was a strike, most youth league pitchers will throw exactly the same pitch as last time—at the same speed and fairly close to the same place. He won't always be able to do this, but he will try. (Good pitchers, of course, won't try this.) Therefore, *when the pitcher is ahead of you on the count, set up for the same pitch.* Certainly expect it to be at the same speed, and probably close to the same place. If it's there, swing.

BALLS	STRIKES
0	1
1	1

SET UP FOR THE SAME PITCH HE JUST THREW.

Never swing on 3–0 unless the coach says so. Make the pitcher work. He'll probably walk you, if not on this pitch, then on the next one. If the coach says you may swing at a 3–0 pitch, he means swing only if it is "your pitch" and go for the long hit.

BALLS	STRIKES
3	0

LET IT GO!

Don't try to hit the first pitch unless it's "your pitch." Most pitchers try to get the first pitch over. A lot of hitters just never swing at it. The best thing to do with those first pitches is, set up for

15

"your pitch." If it's right there, hit it. Don't give the pitcher an automatic first strike, but don't swing at a pitch you can't hit well, either. You still have two more strikes coming.

Watch the pitcher when you're on deck. Everybody on the bench should be watching the pitcher, but you should really be concentrating. See how fast and how high he is throwing. See what he throws when he gets ahead and behind. Watch his motion. Try to follow the ball with your eyes. Remember, he will be throwing the same way to you.

Remember these things about "hitting brains." Know your best pitch, and when you're ahead on the count, set up for "your pitch" only. When you're behind on the count, set up for a pitch just like the last one. With two strikes, swing at any strike. Never swing at a ball.

Bunting

Every player on the team should know how to bunt. It's basic even in big league baseball, but in youth baseball, good bunting can be a very powerful weapon. Young infielders don't play bunts too well, and there is a good chance of getting on base.

Bunting to "sacrifice" is not done too often in youth baseball. If you are told to bunt in order to sacrifice, square away by turning to face the pitcher when he starts his pitching motion. Don't step on the plate or you're out! Slide your top hand up the bat about six to eight inches, hold the bat right over the plate and follow the pitch all the way to the barrel of the bat. Move the bat up or down, depending upon where the pitch is, but don't swing. Just let the ball hit the bat, or push it slightly to aim it in one direction or another.

After you bunt, forget about the ball and run. Most young players lose at least one step toward first base because they like to find out how their bunt is doing. Don't watch the ball. The umpire will tell you if it is foul or not. Run.

Bunt the ball into the dirt. Get your bat *over* the ball so that the ball goes *down.* The easiest out in baseball—it's often a double play—is the bunt pop-up.

17

Steer the bunt away from the pitcher. The pitcher has the easiest play on the bunt, so try to bunt along the first or third base lines. In fact, on most plays, it is best to bunt so that the third baseman has to make the play. But keep it away from the pitcher.

Never bunt a bad pitch. Even if you could reach first base, your coach would usually rather have you walk. If it's a ball, let it go. *Pull your bat back so the umpire doesn't think you were trying to get it.* The exception is the "suicide squeeze" where you bunt *any* pitch (see page 20).

High pitches are very hard to bunt. Usually you should leave them alone, even if they are strikes. The trouble with high pitches is that you can very easily pop them up. Just pull the bat back when you see a pitch coming in too high.

With a man on second, always bunt to third. If you make the third baseman come in and field the ball, nobody is covering third and so your runner almost always moves up safely. But if you bunt it to the pitcher, the third baseman stays back and gets the runner out.

Bunting for a hit depends on not tipping your hand. Do not let the infielders know you are going to bunt before you do so. This means you *do not* square away when the pitcher starts his motion. You have to wait until you see that the pitch is going to be a strike. Then slide your front hand up the bat as before, move the bat over the plate, and let the ball hit the bat. Bunt down one of the sidelines away from the pitcher, and run. If it's foul, the umpire will tell you. Keep running. *If you're bunting for a hit and you foul one, go back to hitting.* You've tipped your hand, and the infielders are now expecting you to bunt. Swing away. It's a good idea to learn how to bunt for a "sacrifice" before you try to bunt for a hit.

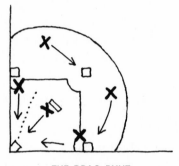

THE DRAG BUNT

The drag bunt occurs when you square away to bunt and then poke at the ball. You should poke it toward where the shortstop or the second baseman normally plays. When you square away to bunt, this is what the fielders are doing: the third baseman comes charging in, the shortstop runs to cover second, the first baseman comes charging in, and the second baseman runs to cover first. The pitcher comes charging in. Notice, then, that there is nobody playing in the regular shortstop position or in the regular second base position. In the drag bunt, you poke at the ball and try to hit it between the charging third baseman and the pitcher—right where the shortstop normally plays.

19

Or you poke it where the second baseman normally plays, between the charging pitcher and the charging first baseman. But the drag bunt depends on all those people charging, so square away and let them know you are bunting.

With two strikes on you, a foul bunt is an out. Never bunt with two strikes on you unless the manager tells you to. If you foul it, it is an automatic third strike.

If you find a third baseman who can't handle bunts, bunt a lot. A poor third baseman who can't handle bunts can mean three or four runs in the game to you. He isn't going to learn how to handle them in the middle of the game. That's why everybody on the team should learn to bunt well. Even the poor hitters will get on base against a team that doesn't handle bunts well. And if you keep bunting against such a team, their whole defense will become very erratic and confused.

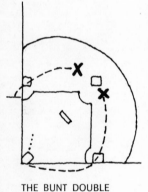

THE BUNT DOUBLE

If your runner is on second, and you bunt and get to first, you can almost always get to second. If they throw for you, the runner now on third will score. This means you get a "bunt double." Stay alert for the chance.

There are times, with a runner on third, when the coach orders a "suicide squeeze" play. This means that the runner on third breaks for home plate just as soon as the rules let him. The hitter's job is to bunt the ball fair and into the dirt. If the hitter bunts, the runner will usually score. The fielders will almost never get him. But if the hitter misses, the runner is a sure out, and if the hitter pops it up, there is an easy double play. The "suicide squeeze" is used a lot in leagues where the rules say a runner can't steal home—or where the rules say the only way a runner can score from third is by a play in the field. Otherwise, the "suicide squeeze" isn't used that often. It takes a hitter who *knows* he can bunt *anything* the pitcher can throw, and it is a dangerous play.

The "safety squeeze" is like the "suicide squeeze" except the base runner on third waits to see the bunt hit the ground. His orders are to score on any bunt hit fair. There is a better chance for a play at home than in the "suicide squeeze" but it's a lot safer if the hitter misses the ball.

The Strategy of Hitting

Most young players should not worry too much about the strategy of hitting. Most players don't have enough bat control to hit the ball where they want to. But it doesn't hurt to know what that strategy is.

Bunting is more effective when the grass isn't cut. Some infields have grass that hasn't been cut for a week. Tall grass on the infield slows the ball down, and a bunt into tall grass will be *more* effective than normal. It's the same with wet grass. So

21

if the game is being played after a rain, or if the grass is thick and tall, consider bunting more.

It is best to hit behind the runner. With a man on first base, it is better to hit the ball to right field than to left field. If it is a hit, the runner will make third. On a single to left, he only makes second. *With a man on second, always try to hit to the right.* Even a ground ball to the right side of the infield will move a runner from second to third. If it goes through, of course, he scores. If the ground ball is to the shortstop or to third base, the runner has to hold up.

With a man on third, and less than two outs, a fly ball is almost as good as a hit. The runner can score from third on a fly ball. It is called a "sacrifice fly" and you do not even get charged with a time at bat. It's scored the same as a walk, but it's better because you win games by scoring runs.

Go with the pitch. Most good hitters swinging for base hits go with the pitch. If they are right-handed, this means they hit inside pitches to left field, outside pitches to right field, and pitches over the plate to center field. Going with the pitch gives you the most natural swing.

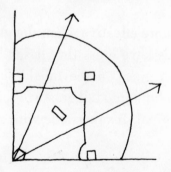

How to Practice Hitting

There is nothing better than regular batting practice. Always try to get some regular batting practice in before a game. Regular batting practice means hitting against a player who throws fairly hard from the pitcher's mound. It's a good idea to hit the first few pitches easily back to the mound, just to get the feel of the bat on the ball. Then swing away.

Play pepper with two or three others. Pepper is a game where two or three fielders stand about ten feet away from you and throw the ball up so that you can hit it. You just swing the bat easily and aim the balls back at those fielders—half bunt and half chop. As you get used to the game, the throwers speed up, throwing the ball for you to hit just as soon as they get it. Sometimes you can even play with two baseballs. It's good practice because you have to swing at everything—high, low, inside, outside—and you keep moving the bat around to get the ball.

Use a batting tee to improve your form. A batting tee is like a golf tee—something stuck in the ground that can hold a baseball on its tip and let you swing at it. A team should have several batting tees at different heights so you can swing at low balls, waist-high balls, and balls around your shoulders. Use the tee to improve the *form* of your hitting. Put the baseball on the tee, then set your feet, focus your eyes on the ball, talk yourself through all the "form" rules, and try to hit line drives. The best place to do this is behind the backstop. Just hit the balls into the backstop. You won't have to chase them as far that way. Rubber-coated baseballs are perfect for this because they won't get scratched on the backstop.

Hang a ball of yarn in your basement and swing at it. Roll a ball of yarn fairly tightly to just about the size of a baseball. Then hang it by a string from a pipe in your basement. Make sure you have enough room to swing a bat, then swing away at the ball. Change the height now and then. But don't just *swing*. Practice your *form*. Practice exploding your hands. Practice swinging level. Some hitters use a bat one size larger and heavier than they usually need, to strengthen their hands. And some hitters swing a bat with a donut on it part of the time to *really* build up the arms. Take fifty swings a night all winter long.

If you're having trouble hitting, get some lob practice. Lob practice requires a pitcher, a hitter, and a basket full of baseballs—ten or so. The pitcher—who can be anyone you know—stands halfway between the mound and home plate and just lobs the balls in, underhand, one after the other. Swing for line drives (away from the pitcher, or you can hurt him). Lob practice is good for your eye, and your form—and it helps build confidence as well, since lobbed balls are much easier to hit than the pitches you are thrown in an actual game situation. After a while, the pitcher can back up to the regular mound and lob the ball overhand from there. Later on he can speed up the pitches. Use a field where the grass has been cut or you may lose a few baseballs in the practice. Fifty swings at lob practice should get your batting eye back.

Get a mirror for your basement. If you can get a full-length mirror for your basement, stand in front of it and practice "throwing" the barrel of the bat right at your own chest in the mirror. (Don't let go of the bat, of course.) If you are aiming the bat at your own chest, you are swinging level. Even major league players practice by the hour, especially in the winter. Explode your hands every swing!

Base Running

There are only two things a team can do on offense: hit the ball and run the bases. Base running is a secret weapon, especially in youth baseball, because every team will get some base runners in every game. The trick is to know how to get the most out of the runners. Speed helps, but brains help more. Slow runners who know how can take extra bases—and score.

General Base-running Rules

Your base coach is the boss. No matter what you think, the base coach controls what you do. If he says "go," you go—without hesitation and without second-guessing him. If he tells you to stop, you stop. If he does not give you any signal at all —or if you are playing without base coaches— then apply the guidelines suggested here.

Know how many outs there are. Base-running strategy changes with the number of outs. When you get up to bat, know how many outs there are. Stop and ask the umpire if you forget.

Know what the score is. With the score 10–0 against you, you shouldn't steal a base and risk an out. With the score 1–0 in the last inning, you almost always should, in order to get a runner into scoring position.

Know who is up. If you are on second and a .500 hitter is up, you don't risk an out by trying to steal. If a .150 hitter is up, you might try to steal third and hope for a bad throw, a wild pitch, or something that will get the run home.

Know the field conditions. Short grass in the outfield means the ball will reach the outfielder quickly. Tall grass means the ball will travel more slowly. Wet grass slows the ball down, too, and makes slippery footing for the outfielder. Look for opportunities to get an extra base.

Be bold. The man who *never* gets caught stealing isn't stealing enough.

With two outs, run on anything. Run on any batted ball, and run as fast as you can. You have nothing to lose.

Draw outfield throws. Run the bases in such a way that outfielders have to throw hard somewhere. Most young outfielders don't throw well and they often throw to the wrong base.

Be alert. Extra base opportunities depend on a split-second lapse by the other team. In that split second, you should take the extra base. You have to be alert, and when you see a mistake, take advantage of it.

Be an actor. Don't tip your hand. Don't let the opponents know what you are going to do. Surprise is one of your big weapons in base running.

Confusion is a great ally. Young players get confused in complicated situations. Confusion almost always means you can get an extra base.

Getting to First Base

When your bat hits the ball, run. Run in foul territory, right next to the baseline. If it's a foul ball, the umpire will tell you and you have as much time as you need to get back to home plate. If it's a fair ball, that extra step you get by taking off *immediately* after the bat hits the ball can be the difference between an out and a hit. *Don't watch the ball until you've passed first.* This is especially true for a poorly hit ball, the topped ball that you're sure will roll foul. Don't stand there. Don't watch. Run.

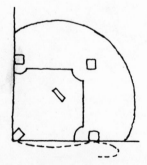

Run through first base on any ground ball. *You should* run full speed *through* the base. *You should not* slow down until one full step *after* you've touched the base.

On a single to the outfield, take the turn. It doesn't matter whether it is a grounder that goes through or a fly ball single. Run as fast as you can to about three steps before first base, then make a small circle in foul territory, hit first base with your inside foot, and take from three to five running steps toward second. By then you should have located the ball.

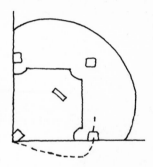

Listen to your coach. If the first base coach tells you to go for second, go. Don't stop to make your own judgment. If he doesn't say anything, *then* make a judgment.

Know what to look for when you take those few steps. Locate the ball. If the ball is on the ground and the outfielder has not yet picked it up, keep going for second. Don't hesitate at all—just keep going. (It will take a perfect play to get you out, so it's a good risk.)

If the outfielder has the ball but looks confused, keep going to second. Maybe he's a good actor, in which case you'll be out. But chances are he really *is* confused and doesn't know where to throw it. Take the extra base.

If the outfielder throws the ball to first base, go for second. The instant you see the ball in the air heading toward the first baseman, take off for second immediately. One of the reasons for taking the turn is to try to fool the outfielder into throwing to the base behind you.

29

If the outfielder makes a wild throw to second, take off for second. Maybe there is a good backup man, but chances are they'll be throwing the ball around for a while. Don't look and don't wait.

How far you go on taking the turn depends on how fast the fielder plays the ball. On an infield hit, don't take any turn. Run *through* the base. Take the turn only if there is no play at first. On an outfield hit, the outfielder must throw the ball to second and the man on second must throw it to first to get you out. If the ball is already on the way into second by the time you reach first, you can take three steps. If the ball is being held by the outfielder, or if he just picked it up, you can take five or six. *Go as far as you can without getting caught in a "pickle."* (If you do get caught in a pickle try to "stay alive" as long as you can. Try to get the defense to throw the ball around. If they do, maybe they will throw it away.) If you take a big lead, the outfielder may think he can get you by throwing all the way to first. If he throws behind you, take off for second.

Watch for the chance to take a delayed double. Sometimes, on a routine single into the outfield, you can take a big turn and then act as if you are going back to first. Then, when the outfielder lobs the ball in, with nobody really paying attention to you, you can head for second. Stay alert. Remember, the other team's outfield generally has their least experienced players—the ones most likely to make mistakes.

30

Take a base on every wild throw. Wild throws are not only bad in themselves, but they cause confusion. The wrong man gets the ball, and the wrong man may be covering second. There may be nobody covering second because whoever was supposed to cover it went after the wild throw. Confusion means you should take an extra base. You'll be out a couple of times, but you'll get a lot of extra bases, too.

If there's a man on first and you single, watch what he does. If he tries for third on your hit, you should almost always try for second. The play will usually be on him. If he's safe, you both get an extra base. If he's out, at least you're on second.

If the play is not for you and the base ahead of you is open, take it. If there is a man on second, and he tries to score when you single, keep going to second. If you hit a grounder with a man on third, and they throw home, go for second. If the play is elsewhere, you can usually get the extra base.

Stay alert for the possibility of a delayed steal on a pickoff. Sometimes a catcher gets very anxious to pick a runner off base. When he gets the ball he may fire the ball down to the base behind you. If your lead is big enough and he fires down, go for the next base. If he tries to pick you off first, go for second. If he tries to pick you off third, you can make a try for home.

31

After You Reach First Base

The very first thing you should think about after getting to first base is *how you're going to get to second*. It must be the most important thing on your mind.

Take a lead as soon as you legally can. The National Little League rules—as well as the rules of numerous other popular leagues in the country—say that you can leave the base when the ball reaches the plate. There are many other leagues whose rules allow runners to lead from their bases as soon as the ball has left the pitcher's hand. Take your lead as soon as it is legally possible. Take three fast, running steps toward second. If the catcher handled the ball cleanly and would obviously make the out on you at second, get back. Don't dare him. (If he's a good catcher, you may be able to take only two steps. Use your head.)

Run as fast as you can on any ground ball. You are forced to run. You have no choice. *Run, even if you are not sure whether the ball is fair or foul.* Ground balls are hard to judge from first base, especially those hit down the third base line or topped right in front of the catcher. If it's foul, the umpire will tell you and give you all the time you need to get back to first.

If the ball gets behind the catcher, steal second. This means wild pitches, pitches in the dirt that get behind the catcher, and balls he just misses—

the ones that go all the way to the backstop as well as those that go just a few inches behind him. If you have a two- or three-step running start (which you should have on every pitch), and if the ball gets behind the catcher, it will take a difficult, perfect play by everybody to get you. Nine times out of ten you can get to second easily.

Steal second if the manager tells you to. The strategy of the game may call for a steal, even if there is only one chance in three that you will make it (and in youth baseball your odds of making it are almost always that good). If the manager or the coach signals you to head for second, go—no questions asked. A signal from the manager or coach overrides any of your own plans.

The delayed steal usually takes a good actor. Sometimes, in the routine of a game, the catcher starts lobbing the ball back to the pitcher even though you are on first base. Take your three running steps and go back to first. If the catcher lobs the ball to the pitcher again, this time you take your three running steps and *don't* go back to first but head for second. This play rarely works more than once a game.

On a single that goes to right field, always go from first to third. On ground balls that get through the right side of the infield and on line drive base hits to right, if the ball gets into right field safely you should go to third. It's a long throw for the right fielder and you will make it nine

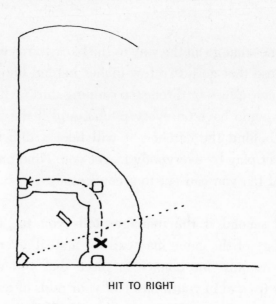

HIT TO RIGHT

times out of ten. Besides, the hitter is probably expecting you to try for third, and *he's* going for second. *On a single that goes to left field, take the turn at second and three to five steps.* If the left fielder throws to second, take off for third. *And on a single that goes to center field, you might go to third or you might only take the turn.* The center fielder is usually the other team's best outfielder. If the ball is in left center and deep, go for third. Use your judgment.

If there is a play on you at second, third, or home, slide. If the play is on another man, go in standing up. But if the play is on *you*, always slide—and always feet first. Head-first slides are dangerous. When you slide, get your foot on the base and *keep it there.* Let the umpire call you out. If you take your foot off the base when you get up, the fielder can still tag you out. Watch out for this second tag.

34

If you're on first and someone else is on second, do what he does. Keep one base behind him. If he steals third, you steal second. If he tries for an extra base on a wild throw, you do, too. If he tries to score from second on a single, you try for third. This is very important. The play is almost always on the lead runner. In some situations, the strategy calls for the lead runner to take large risks only because you are right behind him.

You can go from first to third on a bunt. Often on a bunt, especially one that the third baseman has to handle, *nobody is covering third.* Just keep going to third. Bunts are always difficult to handle. The third baseman has to run in, pick up the bunt, make a good throw to first, then run back to his base and get a good throw from the first baseman who usually isn't even alert to the play. At the beginning of the season especially, this almost always works.

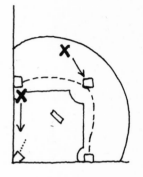

On a fly ball, go halfway to second and see if the outfielder makes the catch. If the outfielder makes the catch, run back to first. If he drops it, you can almost always get to third if you've gone halfway.

After You Reach Second Base

The very first thing you should think about after getting to second base is *how you're going to get to third.* It must be the most important thing on your mind.

Take running steps toward third on every pitch.
On fly balls, go halfway. If you are forced, run
on any ground ball. Do what the runner ahead of
you does. With two outs, run on any batted ball.

**Know what to do if a ground ball is hit when you
are on second and not forced.** If the grounder is
behind you to the right side of the infield, go for
third. If it is in front of you (third or shortstop),
hold up three or four steps off second. If the fielder
makes the throw to first to get the hitter, go for
third. But wait until you see the ball in the air.
Otherwise, stay on second and your hitter will be
safe at first. If the ball is hit in front of you, and
you are holding up three or four steps off second,
be sure nobody is sneaking in behind you to cover
second. Stay alert or you may be trapped off
second.

On any base hit to the outfield, try for home. You
are in scoring position when you reach second,
and unless the ball is hit to the very short outfield
you should almost always try to score. A single
into the outfield will take a perfect, long throw
and a good play by the catcher to get you. You
should also try to score on ground balls that go
through to the outfield. Come in sliding unless the
on-deck batter is signaling you to come in standing up.

**Don't steal third unless the ball really gets away
from the catcher.** From catcher to the third baseman is a much shorter throw than from catcher

to the second baseman. If the ball gets just a few inches behind the catcher, don't steal. If it really gets away from him, then of course get the extra base.

After each pitch, take a longer lead off second than you would off first. The shortstop or second baseman has to run from his position to take a pickoff throw. Many young ballplayers don't even do it, so your lead is perfectly safe. But even those who do, take time getting there; and so you can get a longer lead and still get back. Watch out for the center fielder—as well as the second baseman and shortstop—sneaking in to take the pickoff throw.

On any bunt, go to third. The purpose of the bunt is to move you to third. Whether you make it or not you have to try.

Don't get caught in a pickle. On a close play, you're better off sliding than getting in a pickle. And if it isn't a close play, you shouldn't be in the middle of the base paths.

Sometimes on a bunt, you can score from second. Do not make an automatic try for home, but stay alert to the possibilities. Sometimes on a good bunt when there is a play at first, everyone tends to ignore you as you run to third. So take the turn. If the catcher is out of position, go halfway. If nobody is covering third, go halfway. And if you see a chance, you might try to score.

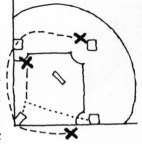

On a fly ball to deep right field, tag up. From right field to third base is a long, long throw, especially if the ball is hit *deep* into right field. Go halfway, but if you see that the ball is going to be caught, run back to second. The very instant the ball touches the right fielder's glove, run for third and slide. Then get up quickly and look around. If the outfielder drops the ball, you can probably score. If he makes the catch, he has to make a long, perfect throw to get you.

If there's a runner on third tagging up, you should tag up if you think the ball will be caught. The play will usually be at home. Go back to the base, and the instant the ball touches the fielder's glove head for third. But make sure that the runner on third is tagging up. Otherwise you will both end up on third and one of you will be out. If you think the ball might drop in for a hit, go halfway even though the runner on third is tagging up. Then if the ball does drop in, you will both score.

After You Reach Third Base

The very first thing you should think about after getting to third base is *how you're going to get home*. It must be the most important thing on your mind.

Be sure of the rules. In some leagues, the rule says that there must be a fielding play before you can score—so you *can't* score on a wild pitch.

38

Know the rules of your league on this. If you don't know, ask your coach.

Stealing home can be very easy—or very hard. It depends on the league, the rules, the quality of the catcher, the alertness of the pitcher, and the distance between the catcher and the backstop. If the league is good, the catcher good, the pitcher alert, the backstop fairly close behind the catcher, it's almost impossible to steal home. The catcher can get a wild pitch and throw it to the pitcher covering home very quickly. The best thing to do is to use judgment and follow the fundamentals—lead off the base as soon as you can, every pitch, and stay alert for the chance. If the ball gets behind the catcher—and your league's rules permit—then use your judgment on whether to come in or not.

Delayed steal of home is sometimes possible. Occasionally a very relaxed catcher might lob the throw back to the pitcher when nobody is paying attention. You can steal on the lob throw if your league's rules permit. This will probably not work more than once a season and the risk is so high that it is usually not a very good play.

If you're forced, run on any grounder. You have no choice. Run for home, and—unless signaled to come in standing up—slide. *Always run in foul territory.* If you get hit by a batted ball in fair territory, you're *out.* But if you get hit in foul territory, it's a foul. Run outside the base line.

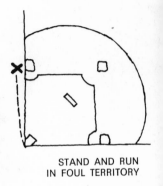

STAND AND RUN
IN FOUL TERRITORY

When you're on third, with a runner on second and less than two outs, run on any grounder. Do it even if you think you'll be out. Otherwise, they will get the man at first and you will still have runners on second and third. If you run, the man on second takes third and the hitter keeps going to second. If you're out, you are in the same situation as before, except that the play was at the plate instead of at first. If the infielder makes a bad throw or if the catcher drops it, you have the run. Faced with a choice of the play at first or the play at home, you should take the play at home every time and hope for the error.

If the runner on first steals when you're on third, you must watch for a sucker play. The catcher is probably going to hold the ball looking for *you* and let him steal. Or he's going to throw to the second baseman who is playing in close or right back to the pitcher (a sucker play). Watch for it and hold up. Your man gets to second without a play. In these cases, take your three running steps toward home and then go back to third. But if they make the play at second and you've got a good lead, you might try to make it home. It's a judgment play. But watch for that short sucker play and don't get caught.

On a fly ball, tag up. You don't even have to take your running lead off third because if the outfielder drops it, you can score easily. If he makes the catch, you also score, although not as easily. The rules say that you may leave for home the instant the ball touches the outfielder's glove, whether he catches it or not. Watch the ball and the outfielder. The instant it touches his glove, fly for home, and—unless signaled to come in standing—slide.

If there is a runner on the base behind you, never change your mind. If you tag up, he's tagging up, so if you change your mind and go back to third, you are *both* on third. If you steal, he's stealing too. So if you change your mind, one of you is out.

Don't try to score on a bunt unless you're forced, or unless you are working a squeeze play. These are only very short throws and generally you will be an easy out. But if the coach has called a "suicide squeeze" or a "safety squeeze," you have to go. Watch for the signal.

Delayed scoring is often a good idea. If you're on third and there is a ground ball (or even a bunt), hold up until the infielder commits himself to a play at another base. If you *see the ball in the air* thrown to first or second, and you have your good three- to four-step running lead, try to score. But wait until you know they are not tricking you.

If you're on third with nobody else on base and less than two outs, and a ground ball is hit, your job is to make sure the hitter reaches first. If he can reach first, he can probably reach second too. Dance off third so the infielder knows that if he throws to first, you score. Chances are he won't even throw. If he throws, you score. If he holds, you hold. But don't get picked off. If he's worried about you and he holds the ball, then the hitter will reach first safely.

All About Sliding

The main reasons for sliding are these:
> You can stop without overrunning the base.
> You are a smaller target for a tag.
> You have a chance to kick the ball out of the fielder's glove.
> You can scare the infielder.
> Sometimes you can slide away from a tag.

Let the umpire call you out. When you slide, keep your foot on the base until the *umpire* calls you out, not the infielder. *Be sure to watch out for second tags.* When you get up to brush yourself off, keep your foot on the base. Most good infielders watch your foot and if you take it off the base, they tag you even though you were safe the first time. You can ask the umpire to call time out so that you can brush yourself off. But the umpire is the only one who can actually call time out. Be careful.

Slide on your side, not on your back. You won't hurt your head that way, and you get there just a little bit faster. Also, your bent leg will be parallel to the ground so the fielder can't tag you there. *Be sure that you never slide head first.* It's dangerous. And you don't get there any faster than by sliding feet first.

Slide low. Many players slide in a sitting position instead of a stretched out position. This gives the fielder a larger target to tag. If you slide *low*, he has the smallest possible target.

In most cases, slide right for the base. You get there faster that way. The exception is on throws from the outfield. If you know how to hook slide, slide for the base on the side away from the ball. (On a hit to left field, when sliding into third, you should slide on the home plate side of the base. Make the fielder turn around to tag you.) Keep your eye on the base.

If the fielder is waiting for you with the ball, try to kick it loose as part of your slide. It's perfectly legal and part of the game. If he is making a one-handed tag, you can very often get it loose.

After the slide, get up. Don't just lie there. Keep your foot on the base but get up quickly. The play may be somewhere else and you may be able to run and get another base.

How to practice straight-in slides and hook slides is explained on pages 45–47. Know what you can do before the game starts. Everyone should learn how to do straight-in slides first. Then if you can hook slide left and right, so much the better. In a game, never use a slide that you have not perfected in practice.

How to Practice Base Running

There's not very much that can be done for your actual speed. But there are many things you can do—and practice—that will get you from one base to another more quickly and successfully.

Practice getting off to quick starts. Start with your foot on an imaginary base and run ten steps at full speed from a standing start. Then do it again. Make sure that very first step is a full stride.

Practice taking the turn. You can go three, four, or five steps beyond first base normally, but you have to practice to get the right habits. Pretend you have hit a ball to left field. Run as hard as you can on the outside of the base line, make that little loop in foul territory, then go five full, fast running steps toward second, stop short and go back to first sliding. Get up quickly. Do it again and again. Hit the inside of the base with your left foot.

Practice going for the double. There are many situations where a runner, almost from the moment he hits the ball, knows he is going for second. Yet in games, most runners hold up for an instant before heading for second base. Practice going full speed from home plate to second base without hesitating at first, and slide into second. Then get up quickly without taking your foot off the base.

Practice sliding. The best place to practice sliding is in a sand pit. The next best place to practice is on a beach, near the water where the sand is packed down. But wear long pants. If you have a dirt area around your house, that can be used too, but before you start check carefully for glass and rocks and things that could hurt you. Do not practice sliding on grass. And it's best not to practice sliding on an actual baseball field because the dirt is usually too hard.

There are three things you must practice for straight-in slides. The first thing you should practice is your takeoff. Leave your feet at exactly the right distance away from the base so that you can reach the base while going full speed, yet you can still stop. If you start your slide too far away, you won't reach the base. If you start it too close to the base, you will slide right by it. In general, however, it is better to slide by the base than not to reach it. You can still tag the base with your hand. Keep your eyes on the base. Generally most right-handed players slide on their right sides, left-handed players on their left sides. A right-handed player sliding on his right side takes off on his right foot.

The next thing to practice for straight-in slides is *tucking under*. If you slide on your right side, bend your right leg at the knee and tuck it under your outstretched left leg. Touch the base with the left leg sticking straight out. (If you slide on your left side, tuck your left leg under.)

Finally you need to practice *getting low* and *getting up*. On your slide you have to be stretched out, lying down. You have to practice getting up quickly, the instant your foot touches the base—without taking your foot off the base. If you get up quickly, you may be able to take another base. (The tucked-under leg will help you get up quickly.)

Sometimes a hook slide may give you an advantage. In almost every case, a straight-in slide is the best slide for you to use. It gets you to the base quickest. But on occasion, if a fielder is not covering his base properly with the bag between his feet and is off the base in one direction or another, you can hook slide to the side *away* from him. For example, you may be going for third base and the third baseman is taking a throw from the left fielder that is short. He leans into left field and leaves his correct position to get the ball. You hook slide to your left, away from the fielder, on the home plate side of third base. The fielder now has to get the ball and come all the way around to the other side of the base to tag you.

A hook slide is a regular slide two feet to the side of the base and past it. As your forward leg passes the base, stick it out and catch the base from the side instead of straight in. You should still tag the base with your forward leg—not your tucked-under leg. If you miss with the leg, tag the base with your outstretched hand.

Hook sliding requires knowing how to slide equally well on both your right and left sides. This is because you don't know in which direction the fielder will give you the advantage. If you can only slide on one side, go for either the straight-in slide or the hook slide on your "good" side. (If you can only slide on your right side, you would not have been able to make the left slide at third base described above.)

General
Infielding
for All Infielders

Getting ready is an important part of the infielder's job. A ball hit to an infielder is almost never hit right at him. He's going to have to move to get it. And most infielders in youth baseball just aren't ready to move. To get ready, you have to be on the balls of your feet—not your heels—with your legs spread comfortably apart, ready to spring in any direction. Your hands should be hanging near the ground and you should be bent over like a runner starting a race, even if you don't know which way you must run. In between pitches, you can straighten up, but once the pitcher gets ready, *you* must get ready—on *every pitch*. Keep your eyes on the ball, from pitcher to batter or catcher and from there back to the field. Be sure to *make up your mind what to do before the pitch*. Say to yourself, "If a ground ball comes to me, I will throw it to ———."

On grounders, keep your head down. That's the only way you can watch the ball, and you have to

watch the ball *all the way into your glove*. Don't
raise your head until the ball is in your glove.

Keep your glove low. Most of the time keep it
touching the ground, since most ground ball errors
occur when the fielder lifts his glove and the ball
scoots right under it. Keep your glove *lower* than
you think you have to.

Expect bad bounces, and field the ball anyway.
There is practically no such thing as a *good*
bounce on a youth league field. If you can't get
grounders that take bad bounces, you can't play
the infield. If you expect a bad bounce, watch the
ball all the way into the glove, don't lift your head,
and keep your glove low—you will get a lot of
bad bounces you may have missed before.

Get your body behind the grounder. Never field
a ground ball on your side unless you absolutely
have to. Run as fast as you can to line up on the
ball, then move in on it or wait for it, eyes on ball,
glove low, head down. That way, even if you miss

49

it there's a good chance of stopping the ball with your body. Also, you have a better chance to move in either direction if the ball takes a bad bounce. Fielding on your side practically guarantees that you will miss a bad bouncer, unless it skips right into you.

Play the ground ball instead of letting it play you. Generally, on a ground ball, *you* move *in on it*, charging it a little. Take it on as few bounces as you can (fewer bounces mean fewer bad hops). Except for the hardest hit grounders, you can move in, save a bounce, and take charge of the ball with confidence. If you move back or stand still, the ball will handcuff you or bad-bounce away.

Keep the ball in the infield if you can. Making a clean pickup is best. Stopping the ball and keeping it in front of you is second best. Letting a grounder go into the outfield is worst. If you have a chance, stop it.

With a man on base, every infielder has two positions to play. He has one position *before* every pitch and one *after* every pitch. See the individual positions to find out where to go.

Call pop flies. On a pop-up, the first one who calls it gets to make the catch. Call it *loudly* so that other infielders going for it can hear you. And if you hear someone else call "I've got it," move out of his way. If he calls first, it's his ball. *Don't call* *a pop-up until you are sure you have it.* Remember, if you call it, it's yours. This means nobody else will touch the ball, so you'd better be sure you have it before making the call. *If you're not calling the pop fly, cover your base.* With men on base, a dropped pop fly can often be forgiven if you get an out somewhere. This means everyone should cover his base.

Step toward your throw. Nobody makes good throws, especially long ones, off balance. If you get the ball on your knees, *get up* and make the throw. Step in the direction that you are throwing (in the same way that a pitcher aims his front foot for home plate). Most bad throws are made by infielders who are *not ready* to throw.

Don't fake throws. If someone is off base and you think you can get him, pick up your arm and throw the ball. Don't try to fake him back by pumping your arm. It's dangerous and silly.

You should be able to make an out when the runner gets caught in a pickle. When a runner is trapped between bases—a situation that's sometimes called "hot box" or "rundown" or "pickle"—he should be a sure out. (You almost never see the play except in youth baseball.) To get the out, throw the ball to the infielder *in front* of the runner—if the runner is trapped off second base, throw to the third baseman *ahead* of the runner; if he's caught off first, get the ball to the player covering second. Your man at the back base should stand with the base between his feet and wait for a throw. Then he can make the tag. Your player with the ball should *run* full speed toward the base runner, ready to tag him. If the runner stays there, he can tag him for the out. If the base runner turns to run back, your man can make *one* throw to the back base for the tag. It takes just *one throw.* You may fake throws so long as you are running full speed at the base runner. Sometimes you can get him with two or three fakes and *no* throws. Remember, always make the play at the *back* base. Never run the man forward.

If you're on the back base, be prepared to receive a throw and make a tag. Move up to the side of the base that the runner is coming from. Get the base between your legs so that the runner has to slide right between your legs to get to the base. If it's a good throw, catch the ball with both hands, and lean forward with the ball in your glove, so that if the runner hits you, you won't fall over backwards. Always *hold the ball low.* Don't let the runner slide *under* your tag. Make him slide *into* it. Close your bare hand over the ball in your glove and be sure that you have the ball securely before you tag him. Then, with both hands on the ball, you will not drop it if the runner knocks you over after the tag. Make the tag with the back of your glove. Then get your hands out of there.

You may need to make a second tag. If a runner is safe, or if you don't know whether he is safe or not, stay with him and make a second tag. You'll make many extra outs this way during the season. A lot of young runners don't know how to stop at a base. They overslide or take their foot off the base.

Never make one-handed tags. If you hold the ball in your glove hand and try to tag him that way, the slider may just kick the ball out of your glove. It's perfectly legal.

Get set to catch the throw even if it is a bad one. Try to get the ball, even if you miss the play. If it's a bad throw, leave your position and go after the ball. But if it's just a slow throw, you don't always have to run in for it. The ball travels through the air very quickly, even on a soft throw. Most of the time you can wait for it to come to you and still make the tag.

Don't worry about interfering with the base runner—just go for the ball. If there is a base runner and the ball is hit to you, go for the ball as usual.

It's the base runner's job to run around *you*. If he interferes, the umpire will call him out. The infielder does *not* have to avoid the runner. But if you are *not* going for the ball, then the runner has the right to the base line. If you stand in his way, the umpire will call the interference on you.

Make the out as soon as you can. Don't pick up the ball, hold it till the runner is almost at first, and then whip it. If you get the ball early, get set for your throw and make the throw early. Make him an *easy* out if you can.

Talk to the other infielders. Infielding is cooperative. It's all right to talk things over with the other infielders before a play. Don't assume they know everything you do. Talk about it. *Chatter on the infield is important, too.* It encourages your pitcher, and it keeps *you* loose.

When the play is over, stay alert for another play somewhere else. If there is a runner on base, the play is not over until your pitcher is standing on the pitcher's rubber with the ball in his hand, ready to pitch to the next batter. Be alert. You may have gotten one man out, but there may be someone else on base to worry about.

Wet grass and tall grass slow down the ball. Play in closer than you normally would, and try to get to the ball more quickly. Charge it, but watch your footing. Tall grass usually helps the slow infielder. (Some major league teams with fast in-

fielders who hit a lot of ground balls, keep the infield grass very short for home games. Teams with slow infielders who hit a lot of home runs keep the infield grass thick and tall. That's one of the reasons some teams win more games at home than on the road—they control the field conditions.)

If the infield is hard and dry, play deeper. If the field has been baked hard by the sun and the grass is short, ground balls will skip through very quickly. You have to play deeper and expect the ball to get to you sooner than usual.

Find the sun. You don't want to look up into the sun for pop flies. If the ball gets "into the sun," you will lose it. If you check to see where the sun is, you can usually put your glove up to shield your eyes while going after a pop-up. Sometimes you have to go after a pop fly on your side, because it would be "in the sun" the regular way. This is the only time when it is all right to go after a pop fly on your side.

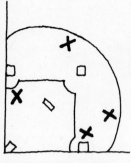

RIGHT-HANDED HITTER

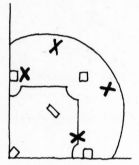

LEFT-HANDED HITTER

To set up for right-handed hitters, the infield shifts in the direction of first base. Generally, in youth baseball the infield sets up expecting the hitter to swing late. For right-handed hitters, then, third baseman plays in, shortstop over near second, second baseman halfway between first and second base, and the first baseman even with the bag or slightly behind it.

To set up for left-handed hitters, the entire infield shifts in the direction of third base. Again, expect the hitter to swing late. The third baseman plays back, even with his base. Shortstop plays toward third, second baseman nearer second, and the first baseman in front of first base.

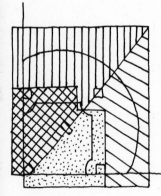

There are certain territories that infielders are expected to cover for pop-ups. Third basemen cover the territory on the *inside* of the infield up to the pitcher's mound, and in foul territory, too. Shortstops cover the territory *outside* the infield, all the way from the left field foul line to short center field. Second basemen cover the area *outside* the infield from short center field all the way to the right field line. First basemen cover the *inside* of the infield on their side, from foul territory to the pitcher's mound. If the pop-up is toward the pitcher, and *if he calls it*, it should be handled by him.

Certain players are expected to cover a bunt. On a bunt, the shortstop always covers second and the second baseman always covers first. Neither of them goes for the ball. The third baseman, pitcher, catcher, and first baseman generally go for the ball, and whoever gets it first makes the play. But bunts should be called, like pop-ups, so that infielders don't run into each other. When the batter squares to bunt, before he hits it the infielders come charging to a position about two-thirds of the way in toward home. First and second bases are covered by others.

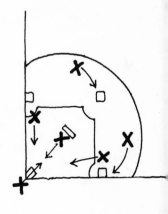

There is one exception: if there is a man on second, the third baseman must decide whether or not he will charge the bunt. If he feels the ball will *obviously* be handled by someone else, he should stay anchored at third for a possible play there. And the pitcher, with a man on second and a bunt, breaks *in* toward the plate and to his right, to cover the bunt on the third base line. If, however, the ball is bunted along the third base line, the third baseman has no choice. He leaves the base to get the ball.

Know who should go after a ground ball. Most of the time it's obvious who should get a ground ball—anybody who can reach it. But once in a while, a ball is hit between two infielders, where either player can reach it. For balls hit between third and shortstop, the third baseman cuts in close and takes first crack at it. The shortstop backs him up. For balls hit between first and sec-, ond, the first baseman cuts in close and has the first try for it. The second baseman backs him up. If the ball is hit through the mound between the shortstop and the second baseman, the shortstop cuts in *front* of the base and the second baseman cuts behind him.

Certain infielders should move on hits to the outfield. First and third basemen *never* go into the outfield to help out. On a hit to the outfield, both of them stay by their bases. But the inside infielders—shortstop and second baseman—should move with the ball. On a hit to left field the shortstop goes into the short left field to help the outfielders, and the second baseman covers second. On a hit to right field the second baseman goes out to short right field to help the outfielder and the shortstop covers second. Notice that both the shortstop and the second baseman are moving in the direction of the ball. Infielders who get the ball in the outfield must return it to the infield immediately. Never hold the ball in the outfield. *Run* it in or throw to the base ahead of the lead runner.

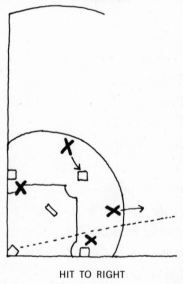

HIT TO RIGHT

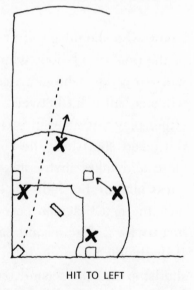

HIT TO LEFT

58

The coach may order the infield in to cut off the run at the plate. This sometimes happens when the score is close. It means that if a ground ball is hit, the infielders throw home to get the runner. All four infielders play inside the base line. The shortstop plays halfway between the third baseman and the pitcher. The second baseman plays halfway between the first baseman and the pitcher. And they all get ready for a throw home.

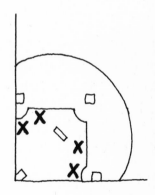

How to Practice Infielding

There are five things an infielder must learn to do—and all of them can be practiced. An infielder picks up ground balls (and bunts), he catches line drives, he makes throws, he catches pop-ups, and he takes throws from other players.

Practicing pop-ups is easy. You need your glove, a tennis ball, a tennis racket, and one other person. Your partner just hits pop-up after pop-up to you with the tennis racket. It is much easier to hit pop-ups with a tennis racket than with a baseball bat, but you will have a little more difficulty catching them because a tennis ball pops out of your glove more easily than a baseball. But if you can catch the tennis ball, you will be able to catch the baseball.

Remember that you line up pop-ups on your nose, and catch the ball in front of your face. If you are having trouble judging pop-ups, get your partner to hit them lower and easier—even just soft "loopers" at the beginning—and slowly build up to high pop-ups.

Practice pop-ups over your head. The over-the-head pop-up is the hardest kind to catch and you should practice those often. You have to turn around and run back quickly, then wait for the ball to come down while you are facing the hitter. Do not try to catch them with your back to the hitter and do not try to run backward. Also, do not try to lope under the pop-ups so that you get to the right spot the same time the ball does. Run back quickly, stop and wait, or even move in again so that you can catch them on your nose. Practice going to your right and left, too.

Practice ground balls with a tennis ball. Stand with your back to the wall of a building. Your partner hits ground ball after ground ball at you with the tennis racket and tennis ball. He hits sharp grounders for which you have to stay back, and easy grounders that you have to charge; grounders to your left and grounders to your right; grounders that bounce two or three times and grounders that bounce the first time right at your feet (those are the hardest to get).

As you get used to picking them up cleanly, your partner should extend your range, making you go farther to your right and left, without telling you where he will hit them. That way, you'll also get to practice *being ready*—up on the balls of your feet, glove low, ready to spring in any direction. You might get your partner to mix in a few pop-ups while he is doing this. Half an hour of this kind of practice is more than enough.

You can also practice by standing close to your garage door and throwing the tennis ball hard against it. The ball will come back quickly and you will have to watch it carefully, all the way into the glove. If you find this practice too easy, move closer to the garage door.

If you can get someone to hit baseballs to you on a baseball field, the best way to practice ground balls is to stand in front of the backstop and let the hitter stand in front of second base. Practice keeping your head down, watching the ball all the way into your glove. And practice getting your body behind the ball. Don't try to take ground balls on your side.

Be certain that you are picking up ground balls using both hands. If you find yourself picking them up with the glove hand only, throw the glove away and practice getting them without any glove (you will probably always use both hands that way). Then go back to using the glove.

Practice catching thrown balls by playing pickle. This is a game in which one runner (sometimes two or three runners make it even more exciting), gets caught between two bases. Infielders on the bases throw the ball back and forth until they tag the runner out. Every base the runners reach safely is scored a "run." This is a good game for practicing throwing and catching, but it is a very *bad* game for practicing how to handle a pickle in a real game. (In a real game, you run the runner back without throwing, or, if necessary, you make

61

just one throw.) Still, if you put the bases sixty feet apart, you will get a lot of throws and it can be a lot of fun.

Practice getting balls thrown in the dirt. All infielders need this practice—especially first basemen. Stand with your back to the backstop or to a fence. Have another player throw the ball in the dirt right in front of you. You should get it on a short hop. Throws in the dirt are not really bad throws. Any infielder can learn to get them if he practices. The things to remember are: don't turn your head away, keep your eye on the ball all the way, and keep your glove *lower* than you think you should. Scooping at a ball in the dirt—that is, swinging your glove hand like a shovel—is usually a bad idea. Position your glove to get the throw.

Practice ground balls and throws. If there are two ball players who can practice together, one throws ground balls to the other who picks them up and then makes good, quick, hard throws to the first player again. Infielders, of course, do this in between innings of a game when they take the field. The first baseman rolls grounders to each of the other infielders and they make throws to first base. You don't have to wait for a game to practice this. All it takes is two players. And if you get into the habit of throwing hard every time, you will probably do better in real games.

The shortstop and second baseman should practice together. The "keystone combination," the shortstop and second baseman, should practice together making throws to each other and running across second base. Having a first baseman roll ground balls to you would be a help, too. The thing to practice is throwing the ball softly, directly over the base, chest high, to your partner who is running to cover the base. There is a lot of timing involved. Don't wait for your partner to get to the base before you throw. Throw to the *base*. Your partner is "coming across" and the ball should reach him, chest high, sufficiently softly so that he can handle it easily, just as he touches second with his foot. You should practice both underhand and overhand throws—underhand for when you are close, overhand when you are farther away. The ball could then be thrown back to the first baseman as in a double play. But the *real* practice is between the shortstop and the second baseman. The more they practice together, the more sure each will be, in a real game, of what his partner can handle.

The shortstop should practice stepping on second and throwing to first. Ground balls hit near second base with a man on first can often be turned into double plays. In such a case the shortstop picks up the ball, runs over to tag second, and then makes his throw to first. But there is a special way a shortstop can tag second that will save one step (and therefore gets the man running to first one step sooner). You will notice that when you throw a ball your forward foot actually touches the ground before the ball leaves your hand. Therefore, if you pick up a grounder, run to a position *one step behind second base*, and just throw to first, your forward foot should touch second base an instant before you let the ball go. But it takes practice. You have to get the feel of where you should position yourself.

Game situation fielding is the very best defensive practice if a whole team is practicing together. In game situation practice, the coach sends four infielders, three outfielders, and his catcher into regular positions. Spare players become base runners. He then fungos the ball all over the field, getting some hits—ground balls, fly balls, and so forth. The runners run as if they themselves had hit the ball. The fielders make the plays they are supposed to make. The coach should be able to set up just about any kind of game situation that he wants to.

If there are sixteen players available, the coach can divide the squad into two teams for game situation practice. One team takes turns running until three outs are made. Then, they change up, fielders becoming runners and runners becoming fielders. You can play a nine-inning game that way in about half an hour, with everybody getting base running and fielding practice. It goes quickly because you have no pitcher, counts, or waiting. Runners stand by home plate and run for first the instant the ball is hit. Most runners cheat a little and start running when the coach starts the swing. That way, the infielders get practice handling the ball *very* quickly.

Catching

The catcher has the most difficult, most active, and for some, the most interesting position in baseball. He handles the ball on every pitch and, in most cases, "runs" the game.

There is one fundamental you must never forget. In practice, in warming up a pitcher, and most especially in a game—*keep your bare hand in a tight fist until the ball hits your mitt*. It's hard to learn to do this, especially if you have played a different position before. But you *must* learn to do it. Otherwise, you will probably break at least one finger before the season is over—most likely on a foul tip. Keep your hand in a fist. Catch pitches with the glove, and after the ball hits the glove, cover it with your bare hand.

Never catch without full equipment. You must always wear shin guards, chest protector, cup, and mask. Many catchers wear batting helmets under their masks, and that's a good idea, too.

Read the pitcher's section of this manual. If your pitcher isn't doing what he's supposed to, tell him.

Give the pitcher a good target. Hold the glove square to the pitcher, not pointing at him. And hold the glove where you want the pitcher to throw: inside, outside, low, and so forth. *Use the target to adjust the pitcher's mistakes.* If you see that the pitcher is throwing higher than he means to, hold the target lower than you really want the ball. If the pitcher seems to be throwing outside, hold the target more to the inside than you really want it.

Don't worry about signals to the pitcher. A young pitcher does not have such a variety of pitches that you *have* to signal them. You can usually let the pitcher call his own game and throw what he wants, when he wants—unless the manager or coach has advised differently. But you can place the target where you think the ball should go. You call the spots, he calls the pitch.

Pace the pitcher. Most pitchers don't take enough time between pitches. When they pitch quickly, they stop concentrating. You can slow him down by holding the ball longer between pitches. But when you throw it back, throw it fairly hard, don't lob it. Hit him in the chest with it. Make it a habit and do it on every pitch. If there is a base runner and you lob the ball back, the runner can try a delayed steal.

Talk to your pitcher. Keep him loose by talking to him, encouraging him. And it is also a good idea for you to *call ground balls for the pitcher.* He is concentrating hard on pitching and often he loses track of other things. You should tell the pitcher where to throw: "First, first!" or "Third, third!" Since you have the play in front of you and can see the runners, you should help him out.

Keep your eye on the ball. Watch it all the way into your mitt. Pretend the batter doesn't exist. This way, you should get all those foul tips.

Keep the ball in front of you. Any ball you can't catch, you must try to block. You must keep the ball in front of you so that you can see what is happening on the field and with the runners on the bases.

Move your body with the ball. If the pitch is outside, move your body outside so that you keep the ball blocked. If the pitch is inside, move your body inside. If it's *way* outside, jump *way* outside. This means you will be moving your whole body somewhere almost every pitch.

The best catcher's position is like sitting in a very low chair. Pretend there is a low chair behind you

and sit down. It's a good position to move in any direction to get a pitch, but it's a hard position on the legs. By the end of the season, you will be able to hold this position for an entire game. Your feet should be apart about the width of your shoulders. You should be on the balls of your feet—not back on your heels.

You don't have to bother with the mask on pop fouls. Leave it on your face if it is easier for you. It doesn't obstruct your vision *that* much, and it is a lot better to leave it on your face than to step on it. A catcher may get only two or three pop fouls a season anyway. It isn't always worth trying to learn how to handle the mask. If you can learn to take the mask off and throw it where you won't step on it, that's okay, too.

Find out where the backstop is before the game. Pace it off. Get in your regular catching position and then pretend that a ball has gotten behind you. Do it two or three times before the game starts. That way you will *know* how quickly you can get there.

Get as close to the batter as you can without touching his bat. If you touch his bat, the batter is awarded first base on interference. But if you stand too far back you will miss pitches, especially low ones.

Call the plays. It is a good idea for the catcher to remind the team what the game situation is. Before the next batter comes up, announce, "Two outs, play to first," or "One out, play for two if you've got it," or "Two outs, nearest base." You should also *call pop flies for the infielders.* A catcher has the best view of the play and therefore can call which of his infielders he thinks should take a pop fly. But the infielder still must call out "I've got it!" if he wants to make the catch.

For a deliberate base on balls the catcher must start in the catcher's box, directly behind home plate. When the manager says he wants an opposing hitter walked on purpose, the catcher stands up behind home plate, in the catcher's box, holding his glove (or bare hand), out as far from the plate as he can. This gives the pitcher a target eighteen to twenty-four inches wide of home plate. When the pitcher throws a medium-speed pitch at the target, the catcher *jumps* over to get his body behind the ball—*every pitch.* (If the catcher doesn't start behind the plate, the umpire in many leagues will call a balk.)

Stealing is generally done on the catcher. In the major leagues, a runner usually steals on the pitcher's motion. But in youth baseball where the rule of most leagues is that a runner may not leave until the ball reaches the hitter (or at least until the ball leaves the pitcher's hand), all the stealing is done on the catcher.

If you catch the ball cleanly and throw reasonably quickly and accurately, a steal should be an out. No runner can go from first to second faster

than you can throw the ball to the shortstop covering second base. You should step toward second base and throw with a little arc aiming the ball right over the bag, waist high. If you catch the ball cleanly, you do not have to throw it hard—just quickly. Take one step and throw.

If you don't catch the ball cleanly, you will have to throw harder—but remember that a ball travels through the air quickly, even when it's not thrown too hard. It is accuracy you should go for, not speed. Never throw until you straighten up to a balanced position and take the step forward. You are more likely to make a wild throw when you throw off balance.

It is better to throw low than high. It is best to hit the shortstop waist high, right over second base. But if you can't do that, it is better to throw low, even in the dirt, than over his head. On a ball in the dirt, he has a chance. He has no chance at all on a ball he can't reach. Throw to the base and don't worry about whether the shortstop will get there. That's his problem.

It is better to throw to the right than to the left of second. Directly over second base is the best place but the next best place to throw is on the side toward first base. The shortstop is leaning toward first and he won't have to lean backward to get the ball.

With two men stealing, go for the lead runner. After every pitch, keep your eye on the lead runner. Forget the one on the base behind him. If there is a play, make it on the lead runner (except for the classic first and third situation, which is discussed on pages 73–74).

Before every pitch, make up your mind where you are going to throw. Know in advance what you are going to do if such and such happens. And *know where to throw if the ball gets behind you.* With men on base, you should try to keep every pitch in front of you, even the ones in the dirt. But occasionally a ball will get behind you. You can be certain, when that happens, that the runners are going to run. Go after the ball as quickly as you can. Throw your mask away. The pitcher is supposed to be yelling to you to tell you where to throw it, but if he's not, pick up the ball, step toward the base ahead of the lead runner, and throw. Someone should be there, so don't wait to look or to see if the runner is going. If the pitcher is yelling "no throw," then don't throw; but if he is yelling anything else—or not yelling at all—throw to the base ahead of the lead runner.

Practice handling bunts. When a batter bunts, the catcher throws his mask away and charges right over home plate into fair territory, even *before* he knows where the ball is. Then he finds the ball and, if he can reach it before the other fielders, scoops it up with glove and hand, and fires to first. Speed in getting out in front of the plate is very important. You should go forward because if the ball is foul, it won't matter. If it's fair, you are already halfway to the ball before you even know where it is.

Learn how to block the plate. With a runner scoring from third and a play at the plate, you stand astride home plate, get the throw, drop down on your knees on the third-base side of the plate, hold the ball in your mitt with your bare hand close to your body, and let the runner slide into you. If you have the ball, you are allowed to block the plate. This means it is all right for you to be on both knees in front of the base so that the runner can't get at the plate. But you can't do that if you don't have the ball.

The runner may try to knock you over and may try to kick the ball out of your glove. You have to hold the ball securely, with your bare hand holding it in the pocket of your glove. When he comes into you, lean forward, tag, and hold on. (Tagging with the glove, if the ball is in it, is okay. But keep your bare hand on it. Then get up and look for the other runners.)

If there is a play at the plate, throw your mask away. Throw your mask to your right, away from the play at home. Sometimes, with a man on second and a single to the outfield, or a fly ball with a runner on third tagging up, you have time to throw away your mask and get the bat out of the way too. With a runner on third on a ground ball, you won't have time to worry about the bat, but throw the mask to the right. If there's a bunt with a man on third, you should let an infielder or the pitcher take it 99 per cent of the time. You should cover home plate.

There is a way to handle the pickoff. After a pitch, a runner on first may be dancing off the base, daring you to throw the ball. Either ignore him or throw to the first baseman. Never fake him back. Sometimes, in the first inning with the first base runner (on the first or second pitch to the new batter), it is a good idea to throw the ball down to the first baseman even if you don't have a good chance to get him. It will let the opponents know that you are willing and ready to throw any time, and will make them more cautious in running the bases. If the runner is stealing, you should throw to second.

The famous first and third steal usually happens at least once every game. The opponents get runners on first and third. The runner from first breaks and if the catcher throws to catch him stealing, the runner from third tries to score.

If there are two outs and you handle the pitch

cleanly, go for the runner stealing second every time. If you get him out—and you should—the run doesn't score. But if you do not handle the ball cleanly—if it pops out of your glove, or the pitch is in the dirt—get the ball and hold it. Let the runner take second, but don't let the runner on third get home. (In certain other game situations, it is more valuable to get the out at second than to worry about the runner at third. If you are ahead by five runs in the last inning, you want outs—you don't care about an extra run. In these cases, go for the runner heading for second.)

But normally, with less than two outs, and when your team isn't ahead by lots of runs, you have a decision to make. If you miss the ball or it drops out of your glove, always forget the man stealing second and let him take the base. Stay focused on the lead runner. Hold the ball. If, however, you handle the pitch cleanly, you can do one of two things. You might decide to make a good throw down to second base to catch the man stealing—the shortstop will get it and make a tag or, if he sees the runner on third break for home, he will fire the ball right back to you. Or when you see the runner breaking from first to second, you might decide to just fire the ball to third hoping to catch the lead runner leaning and off his base. But you can't afford to wait. Don't look, don't fake him back, and don't let him know what you are doing. (You don't want to call a time out on this to talk to the manager because the other team will know something's up.) Just fire the ball to third base right away.

Which of these two choices you use depends on the game situation. In the early innings, the first time this play comes up, make the play to second. In the late innings, in a tight game, or if it's the second time the play has come up, fire it to third. Your fielders should be alert to either choice and both of them should be in position. It is a safer play to either hold the ball or fire it to third. If you are unsure of your throws or if you are having a bad day in a close game, take the safe way out.

For a sucker play, the catcher must be a bit of an actor. With a man on third who is "itchy," dancing off the base and looking for a throw, the play goes like this. On the first pitch, you see that he is itchy, but you don't do anything about it—you don't look over and you don't fake him back. But on the second pitch, you pretend that you are picking him off and deliberately throw the ball over the third baseman's head—right to the shortstop who is supposed to be behind him. The runner, thinking you have made a bad throw, breaks for home and the shortstop throws back to you for the out—or the pickle. If you have him in a pickle, run him back to third base and make the play there.

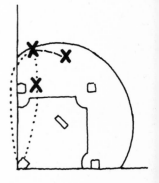

This play usually works better early in the season, before the other teams' players have caught on to it. But it depends most on not tipping off what you are going to do. Don't hold a conference with your manager or coach—just do it. This play works for picking a man off first or second base, too. The second baseman backs up first on the pickoff and you deliberately throw to him. Or the second baseman backs up the shortstop if the runner is on second. But it seems to work best with an "itchy" runner off third.

How to Practice Catching

The catcher is the player who needs the most training. So many of the things he does are not natural that he must practice them often to make them automatic.

Practice crouch and jump off. The best way to strengthen leg muscles is an exercise called "crouch and jump off." The catcher gets into a low crouch, as low as he can get, with his feet apart the width of his shoulders. Then he jumps off to the right to block an imaginary outside pitch.

Then he gets back into the crouch and jumps off to his left. If you are jumping to your right, stick your right foot farther to the right and slide your left foot over. Do *not* do crossovers. This exercise is not only good for your legs but good for blocking outside and inside pitches. A catcher does not move his glove alone. He moves his *body*. And if he's going to get there, he's going to have to move his body *fast*. Fifteen minutes at a time for this exercise is enough. It can be done all winter long.

Practice throws to second. The distance from home plate to second base is approximately eighty-five feet. It is a good, long throw—but a catcher has to make it consistently on steal plays. If you can get someone to pitch to you and someone to cover second base, you should practice taking the pitch, stepping right across home plate with just *one* step, and firing on a line to second. Stand up before throwing. If you throw *quickly*, you won't have to throw hard. Practice getting rid of the ball in a hurry. And remember, throws slightly to the right of second base are better than throws slightly to the left, and low throws to the baseman are better than high ones. Practice throwing from the backstop, too, pretending you got a wild pitch.

Practice scooping bunts with hand and glove. You should pick up a bunt with the same motion that you would use to sweep dirt into a dust pan. Pick up the ball with both hands.

Catch batting practice. This is one of the best ways for a catcher to practice because he gets to handle pitches as if a game was being played. Block the low balls with your body. Move your body in and out for inside and outside pitches. Occasionally throw a ball to a base. And most important—keep your bare hand safe.

Practice pop fouls. Get someone to hit tennis balls straight up. Start from your crouch with your mask on. Then get rid of the mask and catch the pop foul. If you can catch a tennis ball in a catcher's mitt, it will be much easier to catch a baseball, because the tennis ball tends to pop out of the glove. Practice covering the ball with your bare hand once it hits your mitt.

Pitching

In any game, of course, the pitcher is the most important player. Some experts say he is 90 per cent of the game. But in truth, any good youth league ballplayer can be a pitcher if he can throw fairly hard and straight. Pitching can be learned.

Some things don't matter when you pitch. A fancy windup doesn't matter. It doesn't help you throw harder or straighter or anything else. Most youth leaguers shouldn't even use one. Throwing side-arm, three-quarters, or overhand doesn't matter. A pitcher should throw any way he can. Getting the most strikeouts doesn't matter. A pitcher should be worried about getting outs and wins, not strikeouts. Holding the ball a special way doesn't matter. Hold it any way that's comfortable for you.

Some things do matter when you pitch. Balance and control of your body matter. Pointing your toe directly at the catcher matters—there is no way to have good control and good speed without it. When you point your toe at the catcher your whole body helps the pitch. Pitching with your *head*, as well as your arm and your body, matters a lot. Smart pitchers don't need nearly as much "stuff" on the ball. Practice and rhythm matter.

There are some things you should never do when you pitch. Never pitch if you have a sore arm. Never pitch without the correct number of days of rest *for you*. Most leagues have rules about this but they are general rules. You may need *more* rest than the league says. Never throw hard without proper warmup. Your arm and elbow will get very sore if you do. And never throw a curve ball, even if you know how. You can damage your arm for your whole life.

There are complicated reasons why you should not throw curve balls. The bones in your arms are still growing, and most of this growth takes place at the point where one bone meets another—at the elbow, for example. When you reach fourteen or fifteen, after you've had your spurt of growth, these growing areas become fused and strong. But until then, those future bones are still just cartilage. Curve ball throwers in youth leagues often jerk their elbows, sometimes displacing the cartilage. The still-forming bone breaks loose from the bone it is supposed to grow onto. This injury is called a slipped epiphysis.

Throwing curve balls also sometimes causes a fracture in the bone between the shoulder and the elbow—called the humerus—and the breaks

occur just above the elbow, where that snap takes place. The blood vessels to the hand may also be affected.

You don't need curve balls to win games. Don't throw them.

When you throw, "give" the ball to the catcher. The best way to get the right stride and develop the best control is to stand on the pitcher's rubber with a baseball in your hand and then, without throwing it, reach out and pretend to "give" the ball to the catcher. Whatever motion, stride, and position you arrive at when you "give" the ball to the catcher is your natural pitching motion. And that is all you do in the game. Each time you pitch, think about "giving" the ball. This means you should stride well with your toes pointing, reach out, and follow through all the way. You should get the feeling that you are following the ball into the plate. Thinking like this prevents you from releasing the ball too soon (which makes the pitch high), keeps your body straight, and keeps your natural rhythm and follow-through. With practice, it means control.

Develop a "groove." If you pitch exactly the same way every time you throw, the ball should go exactly the same way to exactly the same spot. In the warmups, try to throw every pitch the same way, adjusting slightly until you are throwing strikes. That's the "groove." Everything you throw in the game should be "in the groove" or slightly changed from the groove to fool the batter. But if you need a sure strike, you should be able to come back to the groove any time.

Ignore the batter. You are throwing to your catcher, not the batter. If the batter hits it, he hits it. Once you know what you want to do, throw each pitch to the catcher. *Ignore the runners, too.* Most youth league rules say the runner cannot leave his base until the ball reaches the the batter, or at least until the ball leaves the pitcher's hand. So a runner can't steal on your pitching motion. There is no reason, after you put your foot on the rubber, to pay attention to runners at all.

In general, a low pitch is better than a high pitch. You hear a lot about good low ball hitters. Don't believe it. They usually hit ground balls and these are mostly outs. If they are lucky, they get a single through the infield. The high pitch, however, can be hit out of the park. Keep the ball near the hitter's knees if you can, except when a hitter is trying to bunt.

Adjust for inside or outside pitches by changing your position on the rubber. In the warmups, or even in the game, you may find that your natural motion and natural stride that day are putting the ball a little outside. (Your groove is outside.) Don't change your motion or your stride—just change where you start out on the rubber. The pitcher's rubber is eighteen inches long. Although you start each pitch with your back foot in contact with the rubber, *any* part of your foot can contact *any* part of the rubber. So you may be able to adjust your pitches by just moving over.

Adjust for high or low pitches by changing your stride. You may find that your natural motion one day is getting the ball too high or too low. Your groove is wrong. If your pitches are going high, lengthen your stride. If your pitches are low, shorten your stride. But don't change anything else in your motion.

Start your pitch in front of the rubber. You must have your back foot in contact with the rubber, but you *do not* have to start your pitch standing

on top of it. Most good pitchers dig a little area right in front of the rubber. They start, then, with the *side* of their foot in contact with the rubber, not standing on it. This lets you push off with your back foot and helps your speed. If you start with your foot on the top of the rubber, you must drag it to the position in front. You may not *lift* your foot or in many leagues the umpire will call a balk!

Don't turn your head. When you start your pitch, your eyes should be on the catcher's mitt. Whatever you do with your body, never turn your head or look at *anything* other than the catcher's mitt. Keep staring at it from the time you start your pitch to the end of your follow-through.

Strategy of Pitching

First, get good control. Your first problem is to learn to get the ball over the plate between the batter's waist and knees any time you want it—hopefully with something "on it." Find the groove. This takes practice—a lot of practice. There is more to pitching. But you may spend most of the season trying to get good control, and until you get it, there is nothing else you can do.

Worry most and work hardest with poor hitters. Never let up or relax with the poor hitters. In fact, if you concentrate really hard on the first, second, sixth, seventh, eighth, and ninth hitters in the opposing lineup and never let them on base, you can win the game no matter what the third, fourth, and fifth hitters do to your "stuff." (Some teams put good hitters in the first and second spots, too. In that case, concentrate really hard on hitters in the fifth, sixth, seventh, eighth, and ninth spots.) This strategy is simple. Good hitters will probably get some hits off any pitcher. Don't worry about them. You win games by getting poor hitters out.

"Work" on the good hitters. Try not to throw two consecutive pitches at the same speed to the same place. Good hitters set up for a pitch. After a strike, they are expecting you to come back with the same pitch you just threw, and they have their timing set. Don't do it. *Change speed every pitch.* Change your "spot" with every pitch.

If you get ahead of a good hitter there's a good chance you can get him out. If you get two strikes, no balls, on a good hitter, you should get him. It won't necessarily be a strikeout, but you should get the out. After all, *you have four pitches left.* And *nobody* hits a bad pitch well. Perhaps you'll give him one a foot outside, and maybe he'll go for it. If he doesn't, you still have three pitches left. Give him a change-up that is too high— maybe he'll bite. If he doesn't, you have two pitches left. Don't rush to get him out when you're ahead of him on the count. Use your pitches well. *The secret of pitching is getting good hitters to hit bad pitches, and getting poor hitters out every time.*

Go over the other team's lineup with your manager before the game. Find out who the good hitters are. Numbers three and four in the lineup are usually the best hitters. Talk to the manager between innings to find out who is coming up next inning. *Always know the man to whom you are pitching.* At the very least know where in the lineup he bats. If you are confused ask your manager.

Try to get your first pitch over. Many young hitters (often more than half of them) let the first pitch go by. They want to get a look before they swing. Let them get a look at a strike. Then, if you're pitching to a good hitter, you'll be ahead of him.

If you expect a bunt, pitch high. Keep it in the strike zone, however. It is hard for the hitter to bunt a high pitch, and he will most likely pop it up.

Keep thinking. Pitching is not a machinelike job. You can beat the other team with your brains if you use them. Take your time on the mound. Think of what you want to do with the pitch before you throw it. If you have pretty good basic control, and you keep thinking, you won't need much speed or "stuff" to win. (You may not get a lot of strikeouts, but you will win a lot of ball games and that's what counts.)

Be a little bit of an actor. Try to throw all speeds from the same motion, but it's okay to ham it up a bit. Once a very successful pitcher in a tight spot looked hard at the catcher, rubbed up the ball, looked like he was going to try his absolute hardest, then threw a little floating change-up that the batter missed by half a second. Hitting takes timing. If you can throw the hitter's timing off, you've got him. It is not usually a good idea to deliberately brush a hitter back with a tight pitch, just to scare him. But it is perfectly okay to let one of your warmups go up on the screen.

Don't let your pride interfere with winning. Blowing your fast ball past the other team's best hitter may make you feel like a big man, but it will lose you a few ball games. Forget your pride in everything except winning. Don't pitch strikes to really good hitters in tight situations. It's almost always better to throw four bad pitches and get him to swing because he's mad, or walk him. If he hits a bad pitch, he won't hit it well. Don't be afraid to walk a good hitter. But *never* walk a poor one.

87

Fielding the Pitching Position

The pitcher can also be a vital infielder. Ground balls that he gets are played just as if he were any other infielder. But there are a few very specific fielding plays that he *must* make, and a few that he can either make or not make, depending on whether he is a good fielder or not.

In general, the pitcher does not have to take any pop flies. The third baseman and the first baseman can usually get any pop fly over the pitcher's mound. If the pitcher is a good fielder, he may want to take them himself. If so, he must call them, loud and clear.

On most bunts, break straight in after your pitch. If you handle the bunt, call it—loud and clear. The first baseman and the third baseman are also breaking in, and your calling for it will avoid collisions. Remember, if you expect a bunt, pitch high in the strike zone.

Game Situations

On any ball hit on the ground to the left of the pitcher's mound, break for first base—automatically. You do this in case the first baseman picks up the ball and cannot touch first base. He will throw the ball underhand to you as you run across the base. But don't wait to see if the first baseman can make the play himself. You must assume that you are going to take the throw. Therefore you have to get to first before the batter does. This means that you have to start instantly when the ball goes to your left. If you immediately see the play being made without you, don't interfere.

If a runner is caught between home and third in a pickle, cover home. The catcher will be chasing the runner back to third, but if something goes wrong and the runner gets free, you have to cover home for the play there.

On a bunt, with a man on second, or men on first and second, break for the third base line. If the third baseman can stay at third, you may have a play there. The third baseman starts in, but if you have started out correctly to cover his bunt territory, he goes back to third.

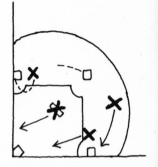

On a pitch that gets behind the catcher, with a man on third, cover home. Some leagues do not allow a runner to score from third on such a play, in which case, there is no need to cover home.

If a pitch gets behind the catcher and there are men on other bases, run in toward home. Yell at the catcher where to throw (or *not* to throw if the man has already taken the extra base). You must be the catcher's "eyes" because he can't watch the runners and find the ball at the same time. But don't get in the way of his throws.

The pitcher backs up third and home. If there is a fielding play at third base or home, your job is to back up the third baseman and the catcher. You must anticipate the play. You know, for example, that if there is a man on first, he will try to go to third on a single to right field. If you see the hit, go instantly to a backup position behind the third baseman.

How to Practice Pitching

Do not throw batting practice. It is a very bad idea to pitch batting practice for your own teammates. The objective of batting practice is to let the hitters hit, and that is a *very* bad practice for the pitcher.

Throw every day, but never—not even in practice—throw if your arm is sore. Some big league pitchers like to throw a little every day. It is a good idea, when your arm is *not* sore, to pitch for about ten minutes every day if you are not scheduled to pitch in a game that day. You should pitch until you feel yourself getting a *little* tired.

Warm up slowly. Make those first pitches of the day easy lob throws. Slowly build up your speed. You should not throw any fast balls until you have already thrown about fifteen pitches. You should use your full windup and your full form even for the lob throws.

Aim for spots in the warmups. When you begin your warmups, throw every pitch over the plate for strikes. Get into the habit of throwing strikes, even when you are fooling around. Then, as the warmups proceed, ask your catcher to hold his glove at a spot—say, knee high at the outside corner—and throw for that spot. When you get three out of four on that spot, get him to change the spot—about chest high on the inside corner. You don't have to throw all your practices hard. The best thing to practice is control. Save the big fast ball for the game.

Practice taking time between pitches. Young pitchers generally do not take enough time between pitches. This could be because that's the way they practice. Even in practice, you should take your time. Think about what you want to do with the ball. Then, using full windup, do it.

Never ignore your form in practice. The form of pitching is absolutely critical, and once you have developed a style of pitching you should never pitch without that style. In your practices and warmups, go through the whole thing—windup, stride, eyes, follow-through, and so forth.

You do not need a partner for garage door practice. If you have a straight driveway, pull the garage door down and mark a box on the door. (You can do it with masking tape that can be removed later without leaving any marks.) Mark the box no higher than your armpits at the top line, and knee high for the bottom line. The box should be about fifteen inches wide. Measure forty-six feet back down the driveway for the pitching mound. Use a *clean* tennis ball and pitch the ball into the box. The tennis ball is a different weight, of course, but you can still practice control with it. After a while, divide the box up into four sections by putting more tape down the middle of the box's length and across the middle of its width. Try pitching only into the low outside quarter. Then, only into the high inside quarter. Cover the quarter you are pitching to with crinkled wrapping paper. That way, you will *hear* when you hit it. Eight out of ten is very good. Use your full windup every time.

Sprinting is especially good for pitchers. Often your legs get tired before your arm does. If your legs were to get tired in a long game and you changed your pitching motion, all of a sudden you might lose your control. Wind sprints—quick starting, running at full speed for about twenty yards, and then slowing down—are very good for a pitcher's legs and stamina. Do wind sprints about ten times each practice.

Playing Third Base

A third baseman in youth baseball needs very quick reactions and the ability to make good, solid throws from fairly long distances. He needs "good hands" because he plays in close, but he doesn't need much speed because his fielding range is small. Still, he's a very important infielder because he gets twice as many balls to play as the shortstop does.

Use the correct fielding position for right-handed hitters. In general, a right-handed hitter cannot pull the ball sharply down the third base line. If he hits it toward third, it will usually be a topped grounder, hit softly. The best position for you to play is about three feet from the foul line and about six feet *in front* of the base. This way, you can get anything hit right on the foul line and you cut down the angle on balls hit between you and the shortstop. If you can reach the ball, cut in front of the shortstop and make the play.

Left-handed hitters require a different fielding position. A left-handed hitter, swinging late, can hit the ball much harder down the third base line than a right-handed hitter can. You should still play about three feet from the foul line, but now play *even* with the bag or just one step in. You do not move *over* from the foul line when changing positions for hitters. You only move in or out. And you should never play behind third base. Stay as near the foul line as you have to in order to get balls hit right down the line, and then move in or out depending on who is up.

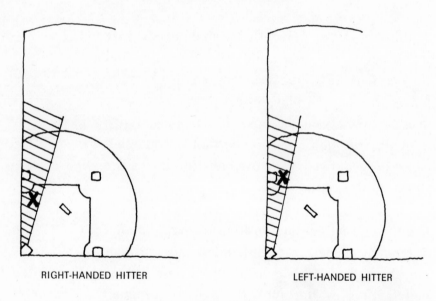

RIGHT-HANDED HITTER   LEFT-HANDED HITTER

Unless there is a man on second or third, you can just relax between pitches. If there *is* a man on second or third, you have to go back to your base *after every pitch.* The man on second might be stealing, or the ball may get away from the catcher and he may have to throw quickly to third, or the catcher may want to pick a man off third. Posi-

94

tion yourself after *each pitch* astride your base, ready for a catch and a tag.

Any ball you are pretty sure you can get is yours. Obviously, any ball hit at you, or between you and the foul line, is your ball to play. On balls hit between you and the shortstop, the rule is if you can get it, it's your ball. But if the grounder is one that the shortstop can get easily, and you would have to make a sensational play to get it, leave it for him. It's a judgment you have to make. If the ball is hit like a rifle shot between you and the shortstop, it's okay to dive for it and stop it if you can. But on a medium-speed grounder, don't wander over to make a sensational play when the shortstop can handle it routinely.

You have a shorter throw than the shortstop, so it's better for you to handle a play if you can. The shortstop is to your left and *behind you.* If you can't reach it, maybe he can, but he has a difficult play on the ball (it's in the hole). If you know you can make the play, cut in front of the short-stop and go for the ball. The farther in you can play, the farther over toward second the shortstop can play, and therefore all the holes in the infield will be covered.

When the hitter squares to bunt, start running in immediately to get the ball. Even before he has hit the ball, you should come running in as fast as you can to a position more than halfway between home and third. Go straight in until you are about twenty feet from home. If he succeeds in bunting the ball, you will be right there.

If the hitter bunts, don't throw off balance. Pick up the bunt, straighten up, step toward first base, and throw it. If you are in the right position, and if you charged when you saw him square away, you will have time. Off-balance throws are almost always wild.

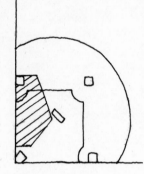

Cover the bunt from the foul line to right in front of the pitcher. If you are in the right position, you will be better able to field the bunt than the pitcher. Except when there is a man on second base, try to cover the whole area from the foul line to right in front of the pitcher.

On bunts, always make sure you get one out somewhere. In many cases with men on base, hitters bunt in order to sacrifice themselves. Listen to the catcher. He will call the play.

Call pop flies, loud and clear. Even if it's your ball, you have to call "I've got it, I've got it," loud and clear, or the shortstop will think it's his ball. *Call bunts as you do for pop-ups.* You don't want to run into your own players.

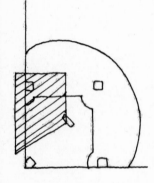

A short pop-up on the left side of the infield (or foul) is generally yours. Unless you have a very good fielding pitcher, you should take pop-ups even when they're near the pitcher's mound. Up to the base line between third and second, you can even take pop-ups right in front of the shortstop. But pop flies behind you, even on the foul line or behind the base line, should be handled by the shortstop. He won't have to make an over-the-head catch as you would have to do.

Remember these general rules: third basemen never go into the outfield to help. The farther in you can position yourself and still make the plays the better. Line up pop flies on your nose and catch them with both hands in front of your face.

Game Situations

If there is a man on first and the batter bunts, generally the sacrifice will work. Most of the time you are better off just playing the ball to first and getting the out. You can take a quick look toward second and if you are sure you can get the runner there, throw the ball to the shortstop covering second. But be sure of getting *one out somewhere.* If you aren't *sure* of getting the runner out at second, make the play to first.

After a sacrifice bunt, run back to cover third base. With a man on first, and the bunt to the third baseman, you should go in and get the ball, make your play to first, and then *run* back to cover third. Don't stand there watching the play, or the runner who was sacrificed to second will just keep going to third and nobody will be covering that base.

You will have to make a judgment if, with a man on second or men on first and second, the bunt is to you. If you come in and field the bunt the sacrifice works since nobody is covering third. (The shortstop has to cover second.) When you see the hitter square away to bunt, come charging in as always. If the bunt is hit so that either the pitcher or the first baseman can field it, you should stop and run back to third—and perhaps get a throw at third. It's a judgment play. If the bunt is right along the foul line, there's nothing you can do except field it and get the out at first.

There are two ways to handle a ground ball to third when there is a man on first and less than two outs. If it's a hard ground ball, or a medium hard ground ball, you can almost always get the force-out at second base. Pick it up and throw the ball to second base (not the second baseman, for he may not be there yet). On a soft ground ball for which you have to go way in, you probably won't be able to get the man at second. Treat it as a bunt and make the play to first. *Then get back to cover third in case the runner keeps going.*

A double play is possible with a ground ball to third, a man on second, and less than two outs. Most youth league runners on second, since they are not forced to run, hold back a bit, then run when you make the throw to first. If the runner is on or very near second base, *make a hard throw to first, then get back and cover third.* Expect him to try to reach third. Be prepared for a slide and

tag. You should get a double play out of it. But remember to throw hard to first.

When you pick up the grounder, look over to second. Some runners wait for you to make the throw by staying about six feet off the base. In such a case, fire the ball to second. You have the man picked off. If he starts to run, you have him in a pickle and he should be a sure out. But *don't fake him back to second.* Pick up the grounder and fire it to second. *Make the play instantly.*

With a man on third, less than two outs, and the ball hit to third, it is usually best to try for the out at first base. Unless you pick up the grounder right next to the base (in which case you could tag a runner who is off the base), "look" him back, then get the out at first. The first baseman will then fire home if the runner tries to score. If the runner is trying to score, throw home instantly.

If there's a man on third, less than two outs, and a ground ball elsewhere in the infield, cover third. The shortstop may make a throw to you there. Or the second baseman might, or the runner may be caught in a pickle.

With men on first and second, less than two outs, and a ground ball to third, pick it up and step on third. If you still have a play at first, fire the ball across the diamond. You probably won't have a play at second, so don't even look for it.

With the bases loaded, a ground ball to third, and less than two outs, play the lead runner. Don't tag third. Go for the man trying to score by throwing home. Then go back and cover your base.

With two outs and a ground ball to third, you have two choices. If a runner is forced at third, just step on the base. Otherwise, make the play to first every time.

Playing Shortstop

Shortstop is the most difficult position on the infield to play because it requires speed, range, a good throwing arm from lots of positions, clean pickups of ground balls, and a lot of baseball "sense." Also, the shortstop generally takes the throw from the catcher on a steal of second. The shortstop must be the most alert player on the team, because he is right in the middle of the diamond and most of the decisions revolve around him. He won't get as many balls to play as the second baseman, but they will be harder to play.

Use the correct fielding position for right-handed hitters. Youth league hitters generally swing late, and their natural power alley on ground balls is toward second. The best place for the shortstop, on right-handed hitters, is shading toward second base, halfway between the base line and the back of the infield. Remember, your third baseman is in close. He has cut down the angle between you and third base. You can, therefore, move over closer to second. You should be in a position where a ground ball hit at a medium speed directly over second base is still playable. You can get it behind second and make the play to first. (A ball hit slowly through the pitcher's box is also playable. You cut it off *before* second base and make the play to first.) In general, on balls hit between you and the second baseman, you should cut in front of the second baseman and make the play. He cuts behind you and gets the ball if you miss it.

Use the correct fielding position for left-handed hitters. You should move about six feet back toward third base. The third baseman is now playing deeper. He isn't covering as much of the hole between the two of you as he does on right-handed hitters. You should play a bit deeper near the back of the infield. Shortstop is the power alley for left-handed hitters. You probably can no longer get well-hit balls directly over second base.

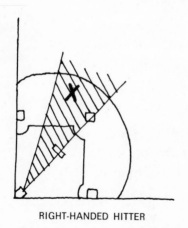

RIGHT-HANDED HITTER

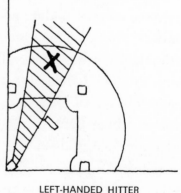

LEFT-HANDED HITTER

Shortstop receives the catcher's throw on steals or pickoffs at second. In most cases, it's much harder for the second baseman to take the catcher's throw, whereas you have the play in front of you. For right-handed hitters, you'll be standing nearer to second base. Unless there is some special reason for not doing so, you should always take the catcher's throws.

With men on base, you have two positions to play: one before the pitch, and one after the pitch. With a man on first, after every pitch, you should cover second in the event of a steal. You must run over, stand astride the base, and give the catcher a target. If there is a man on second, or men on first and second, do the same thing, in case there's a pickoff by the catcher. In this position, you are also backing up the pitcher if the catcher makes a poor throw back. Otherwise, the base runner can steal a base on the catcher's overthrow. With a man on third (or men on second and third, or with the bases loaded), after every pitch you should back up the third baseman in case there is a play at third. The second baseman takes over at second.

On a ball hit to the left side of the infield, shortstop follows the ball. The second baseman will cover second. On balls hit to shortstop, obviously you should go with the ball. On balls hit to third base, you should back up the third baseman. On balls hit to the left side of the infield, you should *never* cover second.

103

On a ball hit to the right side of the infield, short-stop covers second. Notice that you are still following the ball. If the ball goes through the infield, you are supposed to cover second. If there is a man on first, there may be a force play at second.

On a ball hit to left field or left center, shortstop goes out into the outfield. Your job there is to tell the outfielder where to throw, or if the hit is very deep, to relay the throw from the outfielder to the correct infielder. You have to be the outfielder's "eyes." You must look for what is happening on the bases while he is looking up at the ball. Also, if he drops it, you're in a position to pick it up and make the throw yourself. And on short fly balls, you can often make the catch yourself. This is still moving with the ball. The second baseman will cover second.

When acting as relay man, line yourself up with the base the outfielder should throw to, halfway between the base and the outfielder. If the outfielder accidentally throws over your head, the ball should still reach the correct infielder, even if it is just rolling.

On a ball hit to right field or right center, cover second base. If it's a hit or if the outfielder drops the ball, there is a good chance that you'll have to make the play at second. The second baseman will have gone out into right field to help out or to act as relay man.

If you get the ball in the outfield, never hold it there. If everyone is on his base, *run* it in to the infield. Or better yet, throw it to the baseman ahead of the lead runner. It is much safer for *him* to hold it than you.

If a hitter squares to bunt, run and cover second base. You never have anything else to do with a bunt. You cover second—no matter where the base runners are. You never field the bunt, and you never cover third.

A pop fly behind the base line between second base and the third base foul line is the shortstop's ball—if he calls it. The third baseman is in, and would have to make an over-the-head catch. Inside the base line, the third baseman should get the pop fly, even in front of the shortstop. But behind the base line, all the way over to second base, into short left field, into short center field, and behind third base up to the foul line (which is a lot of territory), the shortstop usually has the best play. Get the ball lined up on your nose if you can, *call it loud and clear*, and make the catch.

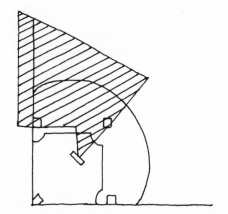

Game Situations

In general, with two outs, make the shortest throw for the third out. On a ground ball hit to the shortstop with two outs, if there is a man on first, your short throw is to second. This is also usually true if there are men on first and second, or if the bases are loaded.

With a man on third and less than two outs, play to cut off the run. This depends on the game situation, and it is the manager's decision before the play begins. If you're six runs ahead and it's in the last inning, don't worry about the man on third. You can play for outs. But in a tight game where one run makes a difference, and there's a man on third with less than two outs, play *inside* the base line and a little bit closer to third than you normally would. (This is because you're so far in that you can't get balls hit up the middle any better than the pitcher can—so you play halfway between the pitcher and the third baseman.) If a ground ball is hit to you, look first at the man leading off third. If he's six feet off and your third baseman is there, fire it to third. If he's more or less on the base, throw hard to the first baseman (because he is going to have to throw it back home). If you see the runner break for home, throw the ball to the catcher. And if the runner is just dancing ten or twelve feet off the base, daring you to throw for him, *run right at him with the ball.* He'll have to go one way or another and you should have him caught in a pickle. It's a

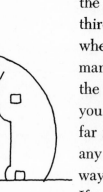

judgment play. But don't wait to make up your mind. Make a play somewhere.

With a man on first and a ground ball to the shortstop, try to make the play at second. Throw the ball to second base chest high. It's the second baseman's job to be there. It's almost always better to throw the ball, even if you are close to the base. (Of course, if there are less than two outs and you pick up the ball just a step from the base, then step on the base and make a play to first for the double play.) Throw *quickly* if you have a chance for a double play, but not *hard*, and always throw chest high.

With a man on first and a ground ball to the second baseman, cover second. The second baseman *may* make the play to you, especially if there are less than two outs. You don't have to tag the runner—just the base. After you step on the base with the ball, *get off the base*. A runner is probably sliding in. Just keep running toward right field.

Sometimes on a ground ball to the second baseman, you might be able to try for a double play. You don't get many infield double plays in youth baseball—maybe two or three a season. But with a man on first, and a ground ball to the second baseman, who throws it to you chest high (quickly, but not too hard), *get off the base, set yourself for the throw to first, and throw.* You can get off the base and set yourself for the throw in the same motion. It doesn't take that much time, but it does save a lot of errors—because *it is very hard to throw accurately when you are off balance.*

On a ground ball through the pitcher's box, the shortstop generally cuts in front of the second baseman to get the ball. The second baseman cuts behind the shortstop and gets it if the shortstop can't. It depends on how hard the ball was hit.

On a ground ball to the shortstop, with a man on second and less than two outs, take a quick look at the man on second. If he's off the base leaning toward third, and your second baseman is covering the base, pick him off. Don't fake him back. He's either off the base enough for you to get him, or he's not. If he is, get him. If he's not, make a hard throw to first base (because the first baseman will have to fire the ball to third).

With men on first and second, less than two outs and a ground ball to shortstop, it is usually best to go for the lead runner. Unless you are *sure* of a double play (and remember, there are usually only two or three infield double plays a year), go for the lead runner. Throw the ball to third for the force-out. (If you get the ball very close to second, and the ball was hit fairly hard, you can be pretty sure of the double play, so go for it.)

The big first and third steal usually happens at least once a game. With men on first and third, and less than two outs, the runner from first steals. If the catcher throws to second, the man on third tries to score. Almost every team tries to do it. There are two ways to handle this play. The first way is for the catcher to throw the ball hard to you in the correct position covering second. You keep your eye on the ball and the corner of your eye on the runner at third. If the runner on third starts home, you take a step in to catch the ball, forget the tag, and fire home. If the runner *isn't* going (which happens most of the time), you make the tag on the man sliding in to you and run the ball to the pitcher's mound.

The other way to play it (especially if it is the second time that the situation has come up in a game), is for the catcher to take the pitch and, without waiting and without faking, just fire the ball to third. If the runner was leaning, he *could* get him because the runner is not expecting the throw.

Once in a while, in this situation, the runner from first *starts* to steal, then stops halfway between first and second hoping the shortstop will try to get him in a pickle and the runner from third will score. You must remember that the man off third is the important runner. Keep watching the man on third while running the other base runner back toward first (normal pickle play). If the runner gets off third enough for you to get *him* in a pickle, you should go for the man off third every time.

If anyone tries a first and third steal with two outs, you should automatically go for the runner coming into second. That makes three outs and the inning is over. There are no other ways to make this play.

You can make a sucker play if the runner on third is jumping around. Lots of youth league runners like to tempt the catcher when they reach third. After every pitch, they dance off third base, daring the catcher to pick them off. The shortstop backs up the third baseman *every pitch*. The sucker play is this: the catcher deliberately overthrows the third baseman, right to you. The runner, thinking there has been an overthrow, breaks for home. You throw home and get him.

The best time to do this is on the second pitch. The first pitch lets the catcher know that the runner on third is leading off the base. The catcher should *not* try to fake him back; he should just return the ball to the pitcher. On the very next pitch, when nobody suspects it and before his coaches warn him, the catcher fires the ball to the shortstop who fires it back. This play works especially well early in the season.

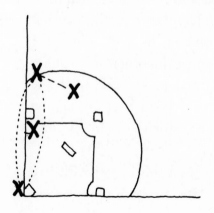

Playing Second Base

Second base is the busiest spot on the youth league infield. More balls by right-handed hitters are hit to second base than to any other position. The second baseman has a fairly short throw and usually has enough time to make his play.

The second baseman's job is to stop ground balls. You have a short throw. If you stop ground balls hit to your side of the infield, even if you don't make clean pickups, you almost always have a play at first. Stop the ball and keep it in front of you. Go down on one knee if it will help you.

Use the correct fielding position for right-handed hitters. Stand halfway between first and second base, and near the back of the infield circle.

Use the correct fielding position for left-handed hitters. Stand in three steps from the back of the infield and three steps closer to second base. This appears to be a shift in the wrong direction, but remember, most young hitters tend to swing late.

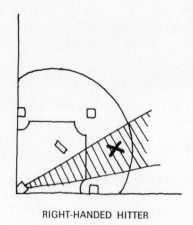

RIGHT-HANDED HITTER

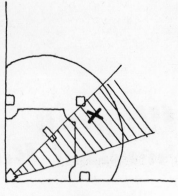

LEFT-HANDED HITTER

Never take a ground ball on your side. If you line up your body with the ground ball, even if it takes a bad hop, chances are you will stop it. You will still have time to make the play.

If a batter squares to bunt, break for first base and cover it. Never go for the bunt. The first baseman has gone to field the bunt, so it's your job to get over to first quickly.

On a hit to right field or right center, follow the ball. Go out into the outfield and help your fielder. He may drop the ball or he may have to relay it. On short flies, *you* may get it yourself. The shortstop is covering second. *But on a hit to left field or left center, you have to cover second.* The shortstop has gone into the outfield to help.

When acting as relay man line yourself up halfway betwen the outfielder and the base he is supposed to throw to. That is the shortest distance for making throws, and if the outfielder accidentally throws over your head, the ball will still eventually reach the correct base.

Making double plays with the shortstop on ground balls doesn't happen too often in youth baseball. You can only make them when the ball is picked up by you or by the shortstop fairly close to second base—about two or three times a season. But if you think you can make the double play, you should certainly try. If the shortstop gets the ball, he will throw it to you softly, chest high, right over the base. You should make the catch standing on the base, *then take one step away from the base, get set to throw, and throw.* Do not throw off balance. Most wild throws result from this. You can get off the base and get set for the throw in one move. But you must get away from the base because the base runner is sliding in. If the grounder is hit to you, throw it softly, chest high, right over second base. The shortstop will get it and he will make the relay. Don't wait for him to get there. Make the throw over the base.

Make throws to the shortstop quickly but not too hard. Try to throw right over the base, chest high. The shortstop is supposed to get there. Throw underhand if you are close, overhand if you are far away. Get rid of the ball quickly, but don't throw very hard unless you have to.

If you get the ball in the outfield, never hold it there. Run it in, or throw it to an infielder who is on the infield.

113

A pop fly behind the base line between first and second is the second baseman's ball—if he calls it. You should try to get all the pop flies from second base all the way to the right field foul line behind first base. The first baseman gets them when they are near the pitcher or in the short infield. But you must call for the pop-ups, loud and clear, or someone else may come crashing into you.

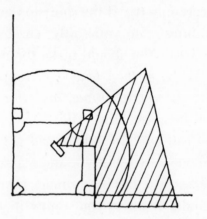

With a man on first, back up the first baseman after every pitch. The catcher might try to pick him off and overthrow. The catcher might want to try a sucker play and overthrow deliberately, straight to you. The shortstop is covering second for the steal.

With men on first and second, back up the shortstop after every pitch. It's a lot of running, but there will be no play at first. If there is a throw, it will be to second or third. You should back up the shortstop covering second.

Either you or the first baseman should get ground balls in the hole between you. If you get the ball, he covers first. But if he gets the ball, *you* cover first—you're breaking that way anyhow. Just keep going and cover the base—as you do on a bunt. In general, on a ball hit between you and the first baseman, you cut behind him—he cuts in front.

With a man on third or men on second and third, cover second after every pitch. The shortstop backs up third. You cover second and back up the pitcher in case the catcher makes a poor throw.

If a play is "busted," throw to first. Sometimes when you're supposed to make a play home or to second or third base, you may fumble the ball. If you don't get the ball cleanly, forget what you were supposed to do and try to get the out at first. Most of the time, because it is a short throw, you will still get the man out.

Game Situations

If there is a man on first and the batter bunts, cover first. Run to first base, take the throw for the out, then fire the ball to third. The man who was sacrificed to second may have kept on running.

If there is a man on first, and the runner steals, back up the shortstop. Unless the manager tells you to take the throw, the shortstop covers second base on steals.

115

With a runner on first, less than two outs, and ground ball to second, get the lead runner if you can. If you pick the ball up cleanly, you should be able to get the man going to second. The shortstop is covering the base. If you don't pick the ball up cleanly, you may still have a play at first. It usually takes longer for the batter to reach first than the runner to reach second. Sometimes you might pick up the ball, tag the runner, then throw to first for a double play.

With a runner on first, less than two outs, and a ground ball to shortstop or third, cover second. The shortstop is moving with the ball instead of covering second.

With men on first and second, less than two outs, and a ground ball to second, try for the man going to second. Or, if you don't get the ball cleanly, try for the man going to first. *You should not try for the force-out at third.* It's a long throw. You could only get the runner going to third if the ground ball were hit very hard and straight at you. And if that happens, you have a better chance to get the double play than to get the man going to third.

With a man on third and less than two outs, the infield may play in for the cutoff at home. This depends on the game situation. If you are way ahead and the inning is late, the manager may tell you just to play for outs. Then you should make the play to first. But in a tight game with a man on third and less than two outs, you may play the infield in to cut off the run at home. If the grounder comes to you and the runner has started home, just fire the ball to the catcher. If the runner has stayed at third, look at him, and then make the play to first. If the runner looks as though he is about ten or twelve feet off the base, waiting for you to throw to first before scoring, or waiting for you to throw behind him before scoring, *run with the ball right at him.* If the man at third tries to go back, fire the ball to the third baseman. If he just freezes and stands there, run right up to him and tag him. But if you have the ball and he's about six feet or more off the base, you should get him out.

With a man on second, less than two outs, and a ground ball to second, don't try to make a play at third. There is nothing you can do about it. Just throw it to first for the out. It's like a sacrifice that works (called "hitting behind the runner") and there is almost no way of getting the man going to third unless he falls down.

With runners anywhere, two outs, and a ground ball to second, make the play to first. Unless there is a force play at second and you pick up the ground ball right next to the base, it is always easier to get the out at first.

Playing First Base

First base is probably the easiest infield position to play, but it's not *that* easy. The first baseman must be able to catch thrown balls—balls that are high, balls thrown in the dirt in front of him, balls thrown into the runner coming down the base line, and so forth. He has to play bunts and pop flies. But he doesn't need much range or speed, and he doesn't need a very strong throwing arm.

Get a first baseman's mitt—don't play with an ordinary fielder's glove. Nobody plays baseball well without the proper equipment. A first baseman's glove is designed to catch thrown balls better than a fielder's glove. It's bigger, making it easier to get those balls in the dirt. Furthermore, it is much safer to make one-handed catches with a first baseman's glove.

Use the correct position for right-handed hitters. In youth baseball, most batters tend to swing late. Therefore, a right-handed hitter could hit with

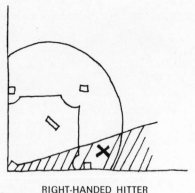

RIGHT-HANDED HITTER

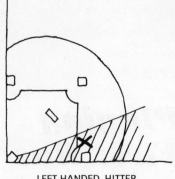

LEFT-HANDED HITTER

some power down the first base line. The best fielding position, before the pitch, is about three feet in from the foul line and about three steps behind first base. You should be able to get any ground ball hit between you and the foul line.

Use the correct position for left-handed hitters. A left-handed hitter will generally not be able to hit down the first base line with much power. You should play even with the base, or even one step *in*, and three feet from the foul line. In changing position, just move in or out—do not move sideways. (If there is a man on first, you have to play one step in because otherwise you will be interfering with his running.)

If there's a man on first, go to the base after every pitch and give the catcher a target. The catcher might want to pick the runner off the base. Sometimes even the pitcher will pick the runner off the base. You must go to the base after *every pitch*. Be sure to get the base between your feet.

Learn to dig throws out of the dirt. In practice, get other infielders to throw balls at you in the dirt on purpose. Balls thrown in the dirt are *not* bad throws. A first baseman has got to learn to get them. And if you practice, with the proper glove, you will see that they are not difficult. You should keep your head down and watch the ball all the way into the glove. Keep the glove lower than you think you should.

On a hit to the outfield, stay on your base. When the runner takes the turn, you must not go with him. Stay on your base ready for a throw. You can pick off careless runners this way.

On a ground ball to first, with nobody on base, nine out of ten times you should beat the runner to the base. In the other one time in ten you will get the ball between you and the second baseman and you will be out of position. The pitcher or the second baseman will cover first base for you. Underhand the ball to him, right over the base, chest high. Time it so that the ball gets there when the pitcher does.

If a batter squares to bunt, charge home plate. Come running in as fast as you can, to a point about twenty feet from home plate (two-thirds of the way in) and try to pick up the bunt. The second baseman should be covering your base. Cover the whole area from the first base line to the pitcher's mound. *Call bunts*, if you've got them. You don't want to run into the pitcher.

121

Pop flies on the inside of the infield are yours.
These include foul pop flies, and some that are
right in front of the second baseman or the pitcher.
But pop flies over your head are usually better
taken by the second baseman who has an angle
on them. It's an over-the-head catch for you. *Call
pop flies you are sure you have.* Don't run into
your own players.

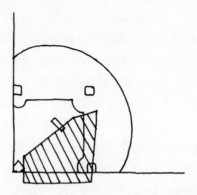

Don't throw off balance. Set yourself, step right
in the direction of your throw, and throw. Most
errors happen when throws are made off balance.

**If there's a bad throw, get the ball even if you
have to leave your base.** Then try to get back to
the base for the out. Or if the bad throw is "into
the runner" and you get the ball, you can tag the
runner coming down.

**Generally, you should get ground balls hit in the
hole between you and the second baseman.** Cut
in front of him and get the ball if you can. He
should back you up.

A first baseman should wait for the throw on infield grounders. Run to your base, put both feet astride the base, stand in a crouch, and give the infielder a target. When the ball is *in the air* and you see it is to your left, put your right foot on the corner of the base and stretch with your left leg. If the throw is to your right, put your left foot on the base and stretch with your right leg. (If the ball is coming right at you and you're right-handed, stretch with your left leg; if you're left-handed, stretch with your right leg.) After getting the ball in the glove with your foot on the base, get off the base to avoid collision.

Never stretch before the throw is in the air. You don't know where the throw is going to be until it is in the air. If you stretch too soon and the throw is high or to your side, you won't get it.

Never go into the outfield to help out. Stay on the infield and cover your base.

Game Situations

With a man on first, charge the bunt. Charge, get the ball, and make the play to first. Let the man go to second on the sacrifice. You usually can't get him, but be sure you get the batter.

With runners on first and second, less than two outs and a bunt to you, generally try for the lead runner. If you get the ball quickly, and if the

123

third baseman has gone back to his base, fire the
ball to third. It's a short throw and you have a
good chance to get the runner out. But if the
third baseman *isn't* back on his base (he came in
for the bunt, too), or if it takes too long to get
the ball, make the play to first. It usually takes
longer for the batter to reach first, than for the
runner to reach third.

**With a man on first, less than two outs, and a
ground ball to the infield, you have to make a
judgment.** If the other infielders make the play
to first, get the out, *then watch out for the man
rounding second.* Some first basemen just fire the
ball to third anyway to avoid taking any chances.
If the runner keeps going, fire the ball to third.
If he rounds the base and just fakes to third, then
run the ball to the pitcher's mound, keeping the
play in front of you. Or look for an opportunity
to pick the runner off second.

**You can make a double play with a man on sec-
ond, less than two outs, and a ground ball to third
or shortstop.** The man on second will probably
hold up, waiting for your infielder to make the
throw to you, and then he will run to third. You
should take the throw, make the out, then fire it
to third. Stay alert.

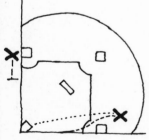

**With a man on third, a ground ball to you can be
handled two ways.** If the man breaks for home,
fire the ball to the catcher. If he doesn't break for
home immediately, pick up the ball and run to-

ward home plate right along the first base line. The batter cannot dodge you. He only has three feet in foul territory in which to get around. Then tag the runner coming to first. You are very close to home now if the other runner tries to score. Any time the man on third tries to score, forget the hitter and throw to the catcher to get him out.

With a man on third, a ground ball to the infield can become a double play. The runner holds up and waits for the throw to you, then he tries to score. Make the out at first, then fire the ball home. It's a standard play and you should be able to get both men out.

First-second-first double plays almost never work in youth baseball. With a man on first and a ground ball hit sharply to you, you may have a chance at the lead runner by throwing to the shortstop covering second base—but don't worry about the double play.

On line drives hit to right field, the right fielder may have a play to first. Cover the base and expect his throw. On other outfield hits, there will probably be no play at first.

Sometimes you should cover home on wild pitches. On a wild pitch with a man on third, some managers like to have the first baseman cover home. Usually the pitcher covers home, but ask your manager. (Some pitchers are good pitchers but very poor fielders.)

General Outfielding for All Outfielders

The big problem for outfielders is staying alert.
You have to pay attention to every man, every
pitch. You have to know the score of the game,
the inning, and how many outs there are *all the
time*. If you have trouble paying attention, here
is a trick you can use: Pretend you are the play-
by-play announcer on the radio and "announce"
the game to yourself. Think to yourself, "Here
comes the pitch. . . . Ball two, low. . . . That
makes the count three and two. . . ."

**Decide what you're going to do before you have
to do it.** Before the ball is hit to you, decide where
you are going to throw it. Say to yourself, *with
each batter*, "If the ball comes to me on the fly

and I catch it, I'm going to throw it to ———. If it comes to me on a line drive, I'm going to throw it to ———."

Don't let hits go through you. On a base hit through the infield or a line drive hit to your position, run to get your *body* behind the ball. Then if you don't pick it up cleanly, you still have the ball blocked and you can keep it in front of you. If a ball gets through you, it means at least one extra base for the hitter, and sometimes two or three. You don't have to pick up the ball the way an infielder does. In most cases you don't have to charge the ball. But you must stop the ball! Don't take the ball on your side.

Never hold the ball in the outfield. Catch the ball or pick it up and throw it right away to an infielder. It is better to throw the ball to the wrong infielder than to hold it in the outfield while you try to decide which man to throw it to. Of course, it is better yet to throw it to the *right* infielder, but throw it anyway.

Throw the ball to third or home on one bounce, and to second on the fly. When an outfielder throws home, he must throw on one bounce, never on the fly. The ball gets home faster if it bounces, and the catcher can get the ball low in case someone is sliding home. And there is much less chance of a wild throw. If you play center field or right field, throw on one bounce to third base also. If you make the throw to second base, or if you are the left fielder throwing to third, it is all right to throw it on the fly.

Throw the ball ahead of the lead runner. If the runner is rounding first, throw the ball to second. If he's rounding second, throw the ball to third. Never throw behind the runner. An outfielder *never* throws to first. (One exception is right fielder, sometimes. See right fielder's section.)

If in doubt, throw the ball to second. If you made a mistake and forgot to figure out where to throw the ball in advance, throw the ball to second. Someone will be there. Just *don't hold it while you try to decide.*

Call for fly balls that you know you have. If a fly ball is hit between two outfielders, and you get there, yell, "I've got it. I've got it." And yell it loudly, so the other outfielder won't run into you. The outfielder who calls first is the one who should make the catch. The other outfielder backs him up. But if you call, you must try to make the catch. Don't call unless you know you can reach it. And listen for the other player's call, too. He may have an easier catch. Then, *you* back *him* up.

With a man on base, every outfielder has two positions: one before the pitch, and a different one after the pitch. An outfielder moves on *every* pitch when there is a man on base. Read the sections on right field, center field, and left field positions to find out where to go.

When catching a fly ball, line it up on your nose.
The best way to catch a fly ball is to get under it
with the ball aimed for your nose. Then catch it
in front of your face—no basket catches unless
you have to, no catching on your side unless you
have to. *Catch with both hands.* Close your bare
hand over the ball immediately when the ball hits
your glove.

Don't lope—it's better to run fast and then wait.
On a fly ball run as fast as you can to the spot
where you think the ball will land, and then wait
for it. If you have to move back a little, or in a
little, you can do it. Don't lope trying to reach the
right spot at the same time the ball does. If you
do that, and your judgment is just a *little* wrong,
you've missed it.

**After the catch, if there is nobody on base, just
throw the ball in to one of the infielders.** If there
is a man on *any* base, after you make the catch
throw the ball to the *base ahead of the lead runner.* It's especially important with a runner on
third to make the catch and *fire* the ball home on
one bounce. The runner may be tagging up to
score after the catch. *Don't wait to see if he is.
Just throw.*

**If the field doesn't have a fence and you aren't
sure where the home run line is, forget about it.**
Catch the ball, and let the umpire decide whether
it is a homer or an out. Some leagues do not even
have a home run line.

129

Use your glove to shield your eyes from the sun.
Sometimes a fly ball hit in the air will get "into
the sun"—or near the sun. In such a case, when
you look up the glare makes it very hard to find
the ball. The best way to handle this is to find
out where the sun is before you have to make a
play, put your glove up to shield your eyes from
the sun, and when the ball is hit, use your glove
to protect your eyes. Make the catch on your side
if you have to. This is the *only* time you should
make catches on your side.

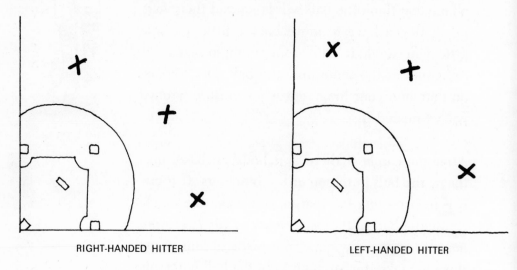

RIGHT-HANDED HITTER   LEFT-HANDED HITTER

**Know how the outfield sets up for right- and left-
handed hitters.** The assumption is that most hitters
will tend to swing late. Therefore, for right-
handed hitters, the outfield shifts over in the direction of right field. The big hole in the outfield
is in left center.

For left-handed hitters, the whole outfield shifts
over toward left field. The big hole in the outfield is in right center.

How to Practice Outfielding

Practice catching fly balls. The way to learn how to judge and catch fly balls is to judge and catch them. There are no secrets. You must practice.

Knowing where the ball will come down really is very difficult. Unless you have fabulous instincts, you will miss a lot of fly balls when you are first learning how to judge them. (The best thing, however, is to miss them in *practice*, and catch them in games.) At the beginning, you just have to guess. With experience the guesses will become better and better, and finally your judgment will be sure.

The best way to practice judging and catching fly balls is to have someone hit a great many of them to you with a tennis racket and tennis ball. Catching a baseball is exactly the same as catching a tennis ball. Decide where you think the ball will come down, get there quickly, and wait for it. Then if you are a little wrong, you have time to move in or out a little. Try to get the ball to come down on your nose, and catch it with both hands right in front of your face.

Practice stopping ground balls and line drives. The worst thing an outfielder can do is let a ball get *through* him. Usually an outfielder does not have to make clean pickups, but he must learn to keep the ball from getting by. He must learn to block a ball with his body, judge how a line drive will bounce, learn how to get fly balls that bounce in front of him, and so forth.

The way to learn to do this is to practice. Get somebody to hit ground balls all the way to your outfield position. If you can only manage to block it, that's still okay. Normally you won't have to charge the ball to make a pickup the way an infielder does. In most cases, you just have to keep the ball in front of you. Get someone to hit line drives that don't reach you, and practice judging the bounce. Get someone to hit short fly balls that bounce before you can get them. Using a tennis racket and tennis ball for most of these practices is fine. And it still only requires you, your glove, a partner—and practice.

Practice throwing home on one bounce. If the ball gets into the outfield and you have to throw home, you must throw on a bounce. Don't throw fly balls that have a large arc. You should throw line drives that bounce once near the pitcher's mound and go right to the catcher. Practice these long throws, but don't do more than ten a day. You'll need somebody to hit the ball to you and to catch it at home plate.

Playing Right Field

Right field is the most difficult outfield position to play in youth baseball. Most balls hit to the outfield by right-handed hitters will be hit to right field, because most young hitters swing late. The right fielder also has two difficult throws to make —to home and to third. Also, *under certain conditions*, the right fielder can make a throw to first.

Use the correct fielding position for right-handed hitters. In general, when a right-handed hitter is at bat, the right fielder should play ten yards in from the home run line and ten yards over from the foul line. This way you are protecting the foul line and playing deep. This is especially true if you have a fast ball pitcher. If there is no home run line, then stand ten yards in from the foul line and about thirty yards behind the second baseman.

Use the correct fielding position for left-handed hitters. Normally, for a left-handed hitter, the

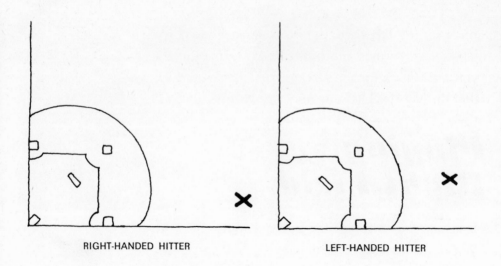

RIGHT-HANDED HITTER   LEFT-HANDED HITTER

right fielder plays right behind the second baseman and fifteen yards in from the home run line.
This way you are playing straightaway and not
too deep. Most youth league hitters cannot "pull"
the ball. If there is no home run line, play twenty-
five yards behind the second baseman.

**With a man on first, the correct fielding position
for right- and left-handed hitters is the same as
above before the pitch.** After the pitch, run to
back up the first baseman in case the catcher
wants to try a pickoff. *Do this after every pitch*
when there's a man on first. If the catcher overthrows first on a pickoff, you should be able to
get the runner as he goes to second.

On a bunt, back up first base. Many wild throws
happen after a bunt. Your job is to back up first
base, *every time.* It is a good thing to do so every
time the ball is hit to the third baseman, but especially on a bunt. Then make the play to second.

Back up the left fielder's throw to second. If the left fielder throws the ball to second on the fly, you must back up the second baseman who takes that throw. Also back up any other throws directed toward first or second basemen.

Game Situations

Know where to throw the ball on singles to right. With a man on second, pick up the ball and throw it home on one bounce. You should also fire the ball home on one bounce if the bases are loaded. In both cases, the man on second will probably try to score and a good throw will get him.

But, with a man on third and a single to right, ignore the runner trying to score. You probably can't get him so play the other runners.

If there is a man on first, immediately throw the ball to third on one bounce. The runner is almost always going to try for third and a good throw will get him.

There's a special case when you can throw to first. If a line drive over the second baseman's head is hit very hard, and if it bounces in front of you once (or, very rarely, twice), you may be able to get the runner going to first. Play it as if you were an infielder and throw him out. You will probably not be able to do this more than two or three times a season. Don't try it unless you know you've got him, because other runners will try to take an extra base on this. Otherwise, with nobody on base and a single hit to right, throw the ball to second.

Use a relay man if the ball is hit too deep. If you recover a ball hit so deep that you cannot reach the infield with a good hard throw, then throw the ball to your relay man—the second baseman —who will have come out to help you. Do not throw it over his head. Throw the ball chest high or lower.

Playing
Center Field

The center fielder is the outfielder who needs the most speed and range. He covers more territory than any other outfielder. He's also in the game a lot because he backs up second base and that's where so many plays take place.

Use the correct fielding position for right-handed hitters. In general, for a right-handed hitter, the center fielder should play in right center field, ten yards in from the home run line. This way you are playing deep and in the power alley for most right-handed hitters who swing late. If there is no home run line, then stand thirty yards behind the back of the infield.

Use the correct fielding position for left-handed hitters. Normally, for a left-handed hitter the center fielder plays in left center field ten yards in from the home run line. This way you are playing deep and in the power alley for left-handed hitters who swing late. These positions are the oppo-

137

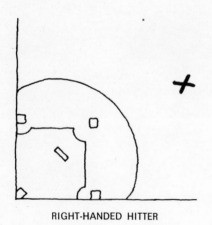

RIGHT-HANDED HITTER

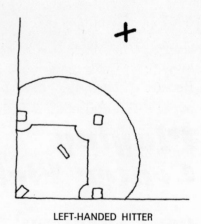

LEFT-HANDED HITTER

site of the ones you would expect, but remember that most young players tend to swing late. Again, if there is no home run line, stand thirty yards behind the back of the infield.

With a man on first or second, the correct fielding position for right- and left-handed hitters is the same as above before the pitch. After the pitch, run in ten yards and right behind second base to back up the catcher's throws to second base. *Do this after every pitch.* You never know when the catcher will make a throw trying to get somebody stealing second, or when he is going to try a pick-off play. If the catcher overthrows, pick up the ball and fire it to third on a bounce. Generally you should back up all throws to second base.

Block the overthrows. If the catcher overthrows second base on a steal or a pickoff, *don't let the ball go through you.* You don't have to make a clean pickup, but don't let it get through you. If it does, the runner gets an automatic base. Keep

the ball in front of you and block it with your
chest or your feet. If you pick it up cleanly, so
much the better—but in any case, block the ball.
Be sure to *back up second base when there is a
man on first* and there is a hit to the infield. You
never know if the infielder is going to try for the
force-out there.

Game Situations

Know where to throw the ball on singles to center.
You should throw to second on the fly when there
is nobody on base (you usually cannot get the
man going to first). Also throw to second on the
fly when there is a man on third since you usually
cannot get the man trying to score.

You should immediately throw the ball to third
on one bounce when there is a man on first.

And you should immediately throw the ball
home on one bounce when there is a man on second (the runner will almost always try to score
from second). You should also fire the ball home
when the bases are loaded. (You usually won't
get the first man scoring, but you will generally
get the man trying to score from second.)

Use a relay man if the ball is hit too deep. If you
recover a ball hit so deep that you can't reach the
infield with a good, strong throw, then throw to
your relay man—shortstop or second baseman—
who will come halfway out to help. Don't throw
it over his head. Aim chest high or lower.

Playing Left Field

Left field, in youth baseball, is the easiest outfield position to play. In most youth league games, not too many balls are hit to left field because most of the hitters are right-handed and they tend to swing late. But just the same, you have to stay alert on every play.

Use the correct fielding position for right-handed hitters. Normally, for a right-handed hitter the left fielder plays behind the shortstop and fifteen yards in from the home run line. This way you are playing straightaway and not too deep. The hitter who can really "pull" the ball has the left field line. If there's no home run line, stand twenty-five yards behind the shortstop.

Use the correct position for left-handed hitters. Normally, for a left-handed hitter the left fielder protects the foul line and plays deep. This means you are ten yards in from the home run line and ten yards in from the foul line. You should be able

to get any fly ball hit right along the foul line. If
there is no home run line, stand thirty yards behind the shortstop.

**With a man on second or third, the correct field-
ing position is the same as above before the pitch.**
After the pitch, run in and over to the foul line to
back up a possible throw from the catcher to the
third baseman. *Do this after every pitch.* You
never know when the man on second is going to
steal or when the catcher will make a bad throw.
If the catcher makes a bad throw and you get the
ball, pick it up and immediately throw home on
one bounce.

Block the overthrows. If a ball comes to you on
an overthrow, block it. Stop it with your glove,
your chest, or your feet—but don't let the ball go
through you, or everybody will get an extra base.
Keep the ball in front of you.

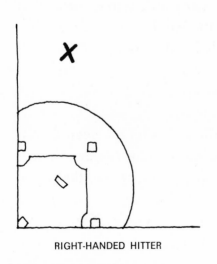

RIGHT-HANDED HITTER

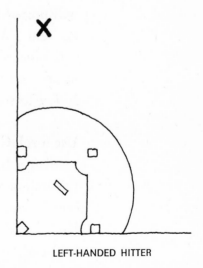

LEFT-HANDED HITTER

Back up ground balls hit to the left side of the infield. Keep the ball in front of you. You should also *back up throws from the right fielder to second base.* You have the best angle to back up these throws. You are the man behind the shortstop who is covering the base. Generally back up all throws to the shortstop or third baseman.

Game Situations

Know where to throw the ball on singles to left. You should immediately throw the ball to second base on the fly when there is nobody on base. Also, throw it to second on the fly when there is a man on third since you usually can't get the man scoring.

You should immediately throw the ball on the fly to third when there is a man on first base.

You should immediately fire the ball home on one bounce when there is a man on second. (He will probably try to score and a good throw will get him.) Also, fire the ball home on one bounce if the bases are loaded. (The man from third will usually score, but you can probably get the man trying to score from second.)

Use a relay man if the ball is hit too deep. If you recover a ball hit so deep that you cannot reach the infield with a good, strong throw, throw the ball to your relay man—the shortstop—who will have come out to help you. Don't throw it over his head. Throw hard, right at his chest or lower.

Coaching the Bases

A base coach is another set of eyes and another brain helping the base runners. First, *read and learn the section on base running*. It is important that you and all the other players understand the same things about the opportunities and risks of base running.

Coaching First Base

The first base coach must make one of three decisions for the batter. The batter could run *through* first base if it was a ground ball and there is a play for him at first. He could *keep going to second* if the ball is in the outfield, still on the ground when the batter reaches first, or he could *take the turn* if it is a single and the other team is handling it well. Be sure to *use both hand and voice signals* to tell the runner what you want him to do.

When a runner reaches first, you are his reminder. You should remind him to get two or three steps

143

off the base just as soon as he legally can, every pitch. Remind him to go halfway on fly balls that will be caught. And you should remind him to run on *any* grounder. *Stay especially alert when there is a runner ahead of your man on first*, because your man should usually do whatever the man ahead of him does. If the runner ahead goes for third on a single, your man goes for second. If the runner on second tags up and runs after the catch, so does your man. On rare occasions, the manager may want the lead runner to do something while the back runner stays put. It is your job to check with the manager for such special situations, since you must tell your runner what to do—or what *not* to do.

You should *relay signals from the manager to the runner* and should *caution the runner* if you see things he should be alert to. Also, it is your responsibility to keep batting and running helmets out of the area around first base—including the area in foul territory where the runner makes his turn.

Coaching Third Base

When a runner is heading into third base, you must make one of four decisions for him. You can tell the runner to stop at third standing up, to keep going for home, to come into third base sliding, or to take the turn. Be sure to *use both hand and voice signals* to tell the runner what you want him to do.

As the third base coach, you must remind and caution the runner who is already there. Remind him to get off the base two or three steps after every pitch just as soon as he legally can. Remind him to tag up on any fly ball. You must also remind him to do certain things covered in the base running section: with men on second and third and less than two outs, the runner should try to score on any ground ball. With the bases loaded, the runner *must* run on any ground ball. With a man on third, on a ground ball the runner should dance off to let the batter reach first. With two outs, he should run on anything hit. And it is your job to caution the runner if you see things he should watch out for.

The on-deck batter is home plate coach. The next batter up tells a runner coming home whether to slide or to come in standing up. If there is no signal, the runner slides.

145

Signals to the Batters and the Base Runners

Some teams run complicated signal systems. Other teams use no signals at all. Occasions when a player should swing at a pitch and when he should let it go by should be understood by every hitter. But if the third base coach is giving signals to the batter, the batter must look at him *every* pitch, just to see if there is a signal. The batter can often do this from the batter's box, but sometimes the batter steps out to get his signal, then gets back in the batter's box. There are usually signals that tell him to hit, take, or bunt. Sometimes there are signals for a hit-and-run play.

If you give the "hit" sign, the batter should swing at *any strike*. If you give the "take" sign, he should *let it go*, no matter where it is. If you give a "bunt" sign, he should bunt at *any strike*. If you give a "hit-and-run" sign, he should swing at *any pitch*, strike or ball, and try to hit it behind the runner. If you give no sign at all, he is on his own. In such a case he should do what he likes, following the rules for hitting with "brains."

The third base coach also gives signals to the base runners. The basic signals to a base runner are the "steal" sign, the "delayed steal" sign, and the "hit-and-run" sign. If you give a "steal" sign, the runner should steal the next base on the next pitch, whether he thinks he can make it or not. If you give a "hit-and-run" sign, he should start running for the next base as soon as he legally can, no matter what. On a "delayed steal" sign, he should steal the next base on the throwback of the ball from the catcher to the pitcher after the next pitch.

There are a number of ways the coach gives signals. The third base coach is supposed to give all signals. They should be given by a *series* of arm and hand movements. You can, for example, touch the peak of your cap, clap your hands twice, touch your left ear with your right hand, scratch your nose with your left hand, hitch up your pants, etc.

147

Usually, one of these movements tells the player to hit, another tells him to take, still another means he should steal—and most of them don't mean anything. And usually there is also a "key" sign. The "key" sign means the first signal you give after the "key," the player must follow. If you don't give a "key," then *no* signal is on.